$\int$IMPLY FRENCH

$\mathcal{S}$IMPLY FRENCH

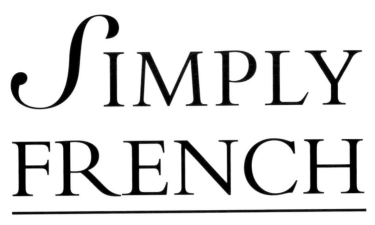

LIGHT, FRESH AND HEALTHY DISHES
FROM A CLASSIC CUISINE

CAROLE CLEMENTS • ELIZABETH WOLF-COHEN

SMITHMARK

This edition published in 1996
by SMITHMARK Publishers, a division of US Media Holdings, Inc.
16 East 32nd Street
New York
NY 10016
USA

SMITHMARK books are available for bulk purchase for sales and promotion
and premium use. For details write or call the manager of special sales,
SMITHMARK Publishers, 16 East 32nd Street, New York, NY 10016; (212) 532–6600

© 1996 Anness Publishing Limited

This book previously published as part of a larger
compendium *The French Recipe Cookbook*

ISBN 0-7651-9732-4

Publisher: Joanna Lorenz
Senior Editor: Linda Fraser
Assistant Editor: Emma Brown
Copy Editor: Christine Ingram
Indexer: Hilary Bird
Designers: Sheila Volpe and Lilian Lindblom
Jacket Designer: Janet James
Photography and styling: Amanda Heywood
Food for Photography: Elizabeth Wolf-Cohen assisted by Janet Brinkworth

Printed in Singapore by Star Standard Industries Pte. Ltd.

10 9 8 7 6 5 4 3 2 1

CONTENTS

INTRODUCTION

The French have the reputation of being bon vivants – *heartily embracing "good living." This is true in the best sense, as, contrary to popular belief, French cooking today proves that eating well and healthily can be one in the same.*

Although classic French cooking may conjure up images of vast amounts of cream, butter and other rich ingredients, French cuisine – the way the French themselves eat – is actually quite wholesome. The French are masters of the savvy use of small amounts of these edible luxuries to create food that is superb and satisfying yet still light. They place great emphasis on good meals, but don't snack between. They focus on high-quality fresh produce, celebrating vegetables and fruits and game and shellfish in season.

The French style of eating in courses is also conducive to healthy living. Enjoyment is as important as sustenance, with smaller portions and more time to savor and appreciate each course. First courses are often fresh vegetables, cooked or served raw in a salad, or perhaps soup. Main courses are likely to be simply-cooked fish or meat with a vegetable garnish. A plain green salad usually follows the main course, sometimes served with a little cheese. Fresh fruit or perhaps yogurt and fruit are typical family desserts, with elaborate desserts reserved for special occasions.

Fresh produce is essential to successful, enlightened cooking and contemporary French cooking really is a *cuisine du marché*, based on the ever changing bounty of the marketplace. Fine fresh ingredients at their peak have maximum flavor and nutrients, and need little embellishment to bring them to the table. The French are prepared to seek out quality and, although the emphasis is on simplicity, whatever time it takes to do justice to the produce is considered worth the effort.

The use of sauces is a well-known characteristic of French cooking that almost anyone will identify. The emphasis today is on leaner sauces designed to develop rich tastes without relying on rich ingredients. Reducing stock creates concentrated flavors, herbs and spices offer enormous variety, aromatic vegetables when puréed give body and texture to sauces. Although lighter sauces are more likely to call for stock and wine than cream, a small amount of cream divided among several servings is a modest indulgence and can be instrumental in blending flavors.

A sauce can be as quick and easy as deglazing the cooking pan with a few tablespoons of wine and perhaps a bit of mustard or herbs, or dousing fresh berries with a little liqueur before serving them.

Fine fresh produce is available in abundance from open-air markets throughout France.

Large Brittany artichokes typify the high-quality produce available at French markets. They are best cooked simply and eaten leaf by leaf.

The following guidelines will help you achieve a lighter, healthier style of cooking:

- Trim all visible fat from poultry and meat.
- Skim fat from cooking liquids before finishing a sauce.
- Reduce the size of portions, especially if you are planning to serve several courses.
- Use lower fat products, such as skim milk, medium- or low-fat soft cheeses, reduced-fat sour cream, low-fat yogurt and "light" mayonnaise.
- Reduce the amount of cheese in cooking by using less of a more flavorful variety, such as Parmesan or Gruyère.
- Use fresh herbs to add flavor and interest.
- Stock-based sauces are leaner than creamy ones. If both stock and cream are used, increase the proportion of stock and decrease the cream.
- Opt for vegetable sauces, such as tomato, or purée the cooking vegetables to thicken sauces.

Relish-like sauces provide a colorful counterpoint to plain poultry or fish and are usually based simply upon chopped fruit or vegetables or both.

Presentation makes a difference and the visual aspect of food is part of its satisfaction. Think about balancing colors as well as flavors. Take a moment before serving to garnish the plate or serving dish – almost anything relating to the recipe will do. The recipes in this book are as appealing to the eye as the palate.

Following the French example can point the way toward fine dining based on sensible choices, not deprivation. Enlightened eating advocates moderation. Don't try to eliminate all fat from recipes, but reduce the amount when possible. Explore lighter main course options, such as fish, game, poultry, and lean cuts of meat. Sauces can add enormously to the enjoyment of food; choose leaner sauces or "slim" them down, but don't completely reject them. Eating as the French do, with more salads and vegetables, smaller portions of meat, and fruit desserts, will also make your meals more healthy.

Simply French brings you a selection of light, fresh recipes for today's lifestyle, with all the flair and panache that characterizes French cooking. Vibrant flavors and creative combinations produce satisfying, enlightened food, as beautiful as it is wholesome. Inspired by the colorful markets of France, with recipes for every occasion, from family suppers to celebration dinners, this book will show you how simple it is to bring this French enlightenment to your own table.

First Courses
and
Soups

First courses and soups play an essential role in a light, fresh way of eating. The French have long known that a simple yet satisfying appetizer or a bowl of soup not only makes a perfect prelude to the main course but also encourages more moderately sized portions to follow. This balancing of the various elements of a meal is an important factor in developing an enlightened lifestyle while deriving maximum enjoyment from food – one of life's most basic pleasures.

ARTICHOKES WITH VINAIGRETTE

Artichauts Vinaigrette

The French enjoy artichokes prepared in many different ways. Simply cooked and eaten leaf by leaf is one of the best ways to savor the delicate flavor of the large artichokes.

SERVES 2

2 globe artichokes (about 9–12 ounces
    each)
½ lemon
FOR THE VINAIGRETTE
1 shallot, very finely chopped
1½ tsp Dijon mustard
2 tsp lemon juice
2 tbsp extra virgin olive oil
2 tbsp vegetable oil
salt and freshly ground black pepper

1 Cut off about 1½ inches from the top of each artichoke. Using kitchen scissors, trim the tops of the remaining leaves to remove the sharp points and browned edges. Rub the cut surfaces with lemon juice to prevent discoloration, then cut the stem level with the base.

2 ▼ Wrap each artichoke in microwavable plastic wrap and stand on a large plate in the microwave or place directly on to the turntable. Microwave on High (full power) for about 10 minutes (7 minutes for one) until tender when the base is pressed; continue cooking at 1 minute intervals, if necessary. Let stand for 5 minutes, then prick the plastic to release the steam and unwrap.

3 ▲ Let the artichokes cool slightly, then, using a small sharp spoon, scrape out the "choke" (the prickly inner leaves and the fuzzy layer underneath).

4 ▲ To make the vinaigrette, place the shallot, mustard, lemon juice and salt and pepper in a small bowl and stir to mix. Gradually add the oil, 1 tbsp at a time, whisking until thickened.

5 Fill the center of each artichoke with the vinaigrette and serve.

COOK'S TIP

Cooking artichokes in the microwave saves a lot of bother. Or, cook them in a large saucepan of boiling water with a few tablespoons each of vinegar and flour, with a heat resistant plate resting on top of them to keep them submerged.

ASPARAGUS WITH ORANGE SAUCE *Asperges Sauce Maltaise*

The white asparagus found in France is considered a delicacy by many, although it doesn't have the intense flavor of the green. White and large green spears are best peeled.

SERVES 6

¾ cup unsalted butter, diced
3 egg yolks
1 tbsp cold water
1 tbsp fresh lemon juice
grated rind and juice of 1 unwaxed
    orange
salt and cayenne pepper, to taste
30–36 thick asparagus spears
a few shreds of orange zest,
    to garnish

1 ▲ Melt the butter in a small saucepan over low heat; do not boil. Skim off any foam and set aside.

2 ▲ In a heatproof bowl set over a saucepan of barely simmering water or in the top of a double boiler, whisk together the egg yolks, water, lemon juice, 1 tbsp of the orange juice and season with salt. Place the saucepan or double boiler over very low heat and whisk constantly until the mixture begins to thicken and the whisk begins to leave tracks on the base of the pan. Remove the pan from the heat.

3 Whisk in the melted butter, drop by drop until the sauce begins to thicken, then pour it in a little more quickly, leaving behind the milky solids at the base of the pan. Whisk in the orange rind and 2–4 tbsp of the orange juice. Season with salt and cayenne pepper and keep warm, stirring occasionally.

4 ▲ Cut off the tough ends from the asparagus spears and trim to the same length. If peeling, hold each spear gently by the tip, then using a vegetable peeler, strip off the peel and scales from just below the tip to the end. Rinse in cold water.

5 Fill a large deep frying pan or wok with 2 inches of water and bring to a boil over a medium-high heat. Add the asparagus and bring back to a boil, then simmer for 4–7 minutes, until just tender.

6 Carefully transfer the spears to a large colander to drain, then lay them on a paper towel and pat dry. Arrange on a large serving platter or individual plates and spoon over a little sauce. Scatter the orange zest over the sauce and serve at once.

COOK'S TIP

This sauce is a kind of hollandaise and needs gentle treatment. If the egg yolk mixture thickens too quickly, remove from the heat and plunge the base of the pan into cold water to prevent the sauce from curdling. The sauce should keep over hot water for 1 hour, but don't let it get too hot.

BROILED GOAT CHEESE SALAD

Salade de Chèvre

Here is the salad and cheese course on one plate – or serve it as a quick and satisfying first course or light lunch. The fresh tangy flavor of goat cheese contrasts with the mild salad leaves.

SERVES 4

2 firm round whole goat cheeses, such as
  Crottin de Chavignol *or* Coach
  Farm Chèvre *(about 2½–4 ounces
  each)*
4 slices French bread
extra virgin olive oil, for drizzling
5–6 cups mixed salad leaves
chopped fresh chives, to garnish
FOR THE VINAIGRETTE DRESSING
½ garlic clove
1 tsp Dijon mustard
1 tsp white wine vinegar
1 tsp dry white wine
3 tbsp extra virgin olive oil
salt and freshly ground black pepper

1 ▼ To make the dressing, rub a large salad bowl with the cut side of the garlic clove. Combine the mustard, vinegar and wine, salt and pepper in the bowl. Whisk in the olive oil, 1 tbsp at a time, to form a thick vinaigrette.

2 ▲ Cut the goat cheeses in half crosswise using a sharp knife.

3 ▲ Preheat the broiler. Arrange the bread slices on a baking sheet and toast the bread on one side. Turn over and place a piece of cheese, cut side up, on each slice. Drizzle with olive oil and broil until the cheese is lightly browned.

4 ▲ Add the greens to the salad bowl and toss to coat them with the dressing. Divide the salad among four plates, top each with a goat cheese croûton and serve, garnished with chives.

ROQUEFORT AND CUCUMBER MOUSSE *Mousse au Roquefort*

This cool and refreshing mousse makes a perfect summer first course. Other blue-veined cheeses, such as bleu d'Auvergne *or* fourme d'Ambert, *may be used instead of* Roquefort.

<u>SERVES 6</u>

7 inch piece cucumber
2 tsp powdered gelatin
5 tbsp cold water
3½ ounces Roquefort cheese
7 ounces full-, medium- or low-fat soft cheese
3 tbsp crème fraîche or sour cream
cayenne or white pepper
seedless red and green grapes and mint leaves, to garnish

1 ▲ Peel the cucumber and cut lengthwise into quarters. Remove the seeds and cut the cucumber strips into 1 inch pieces.

2 Sprinkle the gelatin over the cold water in a small heatproof bowl. Let the gelatin stand to soften for about 2 minutes, then place the bowl in a shallow pan of simmering water. Heat until the gelatin is dissolved, stirring occasionally.

3 In a food processor fitted with the metal blade, process the cheeses and cream until smooth. Add the dissolved gelatin and process to blend. Add the cucumber and pulse to chop finely without completely reducing it to a purée. Season with cayenne or white pepper.

4 ▼ Rinse a 6¼ cup dish or mold with cold water. Carefully spoon the mixture into the dish or mold and tap gently to remove air bubbles. Chill for 4–6 hours or overnight until well set.

5 ▲ To turn out, run a knife around the edge of the dish or mold, dip in hot water for 10–15 seconds and wipe the wet base. Place a large plate over the top of the dish and invert both together, shaking firmly to release the mousse. Garnish with grapes and mint leaves.

13

COUNTRY-STYLE PÂTÉ WITH LEEKS *Pâté de Porc aux Poireaux*

Traditionally this sort of pork pâté (or more correctly, terrine, since it has no crust) contains pork liver and egg to bind. This version uses leeks instead for a fresher flavor and a lighter result.

SERVES 8–10

1 pound trimmed leeks (white and light
   green parts)
1 tbsp butter
2 or 3 large garlic cloves, finely chopped
2¼ pounds lean pork leg or shoulder
5 ounces smoked bacon strips
1½ tsp chopped fresh thyme
3 sage leaves, finely chopped
¼ tsp quatre èpices (a mix of ground
   cloves, cinnamon, nutmeg and
   pepper)
¼ tsp ground cumin
pinch of freshly grated nutmeg
½ tsp salt
1 tsp freshly ground black pepper
1 bay leaf

1 ▲ Cut the leeks lengthwise, wash well and slice thinly. Melt the butter in a large heavy saucepan, add the leeks, then cover and cook over medium-low heat for 10 minutes, stirring occasionally. Add the garlic and continue cooking for about 10 minutes until the leeks are very soft, then set aside to cool.

COOK'S TIP

In France, *cornichons* (small dill pickles) and mustard are traditional accompaniments for pork terrines along with slices of crusty baguette.

2 ▲ Trim all the fat, tendons and connective tissue from the pork and cut the meat into 1¾ inch cubes. Working in two or three batches, put the meat into a food processor fitted with the metal blade; the bowl should be about half-full. Pulse to chop the meat to a coarse purée. Alternatively, pass the meat through the coarse blade of a meat grinder. Transfer the meat to a large mixing bowl and remove any white stringy pieces.

3 Reserve two of the bacon strips for garnishing, and chop or grind the remaining bacon strips. Add the chopped or ground bacon to the pork in the bowl.

4 Preheat the oven to 350°F. Line the base and sides of a 6¼ cup terrine or loaf pan with wax paper or non-stick baking paper.

5 ▲ Add the leeks, herbs, spices and salt and pepper to the bowl with the pork and bacon and, using a wooden spoon or your fingertips, mix until well combined.

6 ▲ Spoon the mixture into the terrine or loaf pan, pressing it into the corners and compacting it. Tap firmly to settle the mixture and smooth the top. Arrange the bay leaf and bacon strips on top, then cover tightly with foil.

7 ▲ Place the terrine or loaf pan in a roasting pan and pour boiling water to come halfway up the sides. Bake for 1¼ hours.

8 Lift the terrine out of the roasting pan and pour out the water. Put the terrine back in the pan and place a baking sheet or board on top. If the pâté has not risen above the sides of the terrine, place a foil-covered board inside the pan to lie directly on the pâté. Weight with two or three large cans or other heavy objects while it cools. (Liquid will seep out which is why the terrine should stand inside a roasting pan.) Chill until cold, preferably overnight, before slicing.

Cold Leek and Potato Soup

Vichyssoise

Serve this flavorful soup with a dollop of crème fraîche or sour cream and sprinkle with a few snipped fresh chives – or, on very special occasions, garnish with a small spoonful of caviar.

Serves 6–8

1 pound potatoes (about 3 large),
    peeled and cubed
6 cups chicken broth
4 medium leeks, trimmed
⅔ cup crème fraîche or
    sour cream
salt and freshly ground black pepper
3 tbsp chopped fresh chives,
    to garnish

1 Put the potatoes and broth in a saucepan or flameproof casserole and bring to a boil. Reduce the heat and simmer for 15–20 minutes.

2 ▼ Make a slit along the length of each leek and rinse well under cold running water. Slice thinly.

3 ▲ When the potatoes are barely tender, stir in the leeks. Season with salt and pepper and simmer for 10–15 minutes until the vegetables are soft, stirring occasionally. If the soup appears too thick, thin it down with a little more broth or water.

4 ▲ Purée the soup in a blender or food processor, in batches if necessary. If you would prefer a very smooth soup, pass it through a food mill or press through a coarse sieve. Stir in most of the cream, cool and then chill. To serve, ladle into chilled bowls and garnish with a swirl of cream and chopped chives.

Variation

To make a low-fat soup, use low-fat sour cream. Alternatively, leave out the cream altogether and thin the soup with a little skim milk.

FRESH PEA SOUP

Potage Saint-Germain

This soup takes its name from a suburb of Paris where peas used to be cultivated in market gardens. If fresh peas are not available, use frozen peas, but thaw and rinse them before use.

SERVES 2–3

pat of butter
2 or 3 shallots, finely chopped
3 cups shelled fresh peas (from
    about 3 pounds garden peas)
    or thawed frozen peas
2 cups water
3–4 tbsp whipping cream
    (optional)
salt and freshly ground black pepper
croûtons or crumbled crisp bacon,
    to garnish

3 ▲ When the peas are tender, ladle them into a food processor or blender with a little of the cooking liquid and process until smooth.

4 ▼ Strain the soup into the saucepan or casserole, stir in the cream, if using, and heat through without boiling. Add seasoning and serve hot, garnished with croûtons or bacon.

1 ▲ Melt the butter in a heavy saucepan or flameproof casserole. Add the shallots and cook for about 3 minutes, stirring occasionally.

2 ▲ Add the peas and water and season with salt and a little pepper. Cover and simmer for about 12 minutes for young or frozen peas and up to 18 minutes for large or older peas, stirring occasionally.

SUMMER TOMATO SOUP

Soupe de Tomates Fraîches

The success of this soup depends on having ripe, full-flavored tomatoes, such as the plum variety, so make it when the tomato season is at its peak. It is equally delicious served cold.

SERVES 4

1 tbsp olive oil
1 large onion, chopped
1 carrot, chopped
2¼ pounds ripe tomatoes, cored and
    quartered
2 garlic cloves, chopped
5 thyme sprigs, or ¼ tsp dried
    thyme
4 or 5 marjoram sprigs, or ¼ tsp
    dried marjoram
1 bay leaf
3 tbsp crème fraîche, sour cream
    or yogurt, plus a little extra
    to garnish
salt and freshly ground black pepper

1 Heat the olive oil in a large preferably stainless steel saucepan or flameproof casserole.

2 ▼ Add the onion and carrot and cook over a medium heat for 3–4 minutes, until just softened, stirring occasionally.

VARIATION

To serve the soup cold, omit the cream or yogurt and leave to cool, then chill.

3 ▲ Add the tomatoes, garlic and herbs. Reduce the heat and simmer, covered, for 30 minutes.

4 Pass the soup through a food mill or press through a sieve into the pan. Stir in the cream or yogurt and season. Reheat gently and serve garnished with a spoonful of cream or yogurt and a sprig of marjoram.

PUMPKIN SOUP

Crème de Citrouille

When the first frosts of autumn chill the air, large bright orange pumpkins are a vivid sight at local markets all over France and provide the basis for some warm and comforting soups.

SERVES 6–8

2 tbsp butter
1 large onion, chopped
2 shallots, chopped
2 medium potatoes, peeled and cubed
6 cups cubed pumpkin
8 cups chicken or vegetable broth
½ tsp ground cumin
pinch of ground nutmeg
salt and freshly ground black pepper
fresh parsley or chives, to garnish

1 Melt the butter in a large saucepan. Add the onion and shallots to the pan and cook for 4–5 minutes until just softened.

2 ▲ Add the potatoes, pumpkin, broth and spices to the pan, and season with a little salt and black pepper. Reduce the heat to low and simmer, covered, for about 1 hour, stirring occasionally.

3 ▼ With a slotted spoon, transfer the cooked vegetables to a food processor and process until smooth, adding a little of the cooking liquid if needed. Return the purée to the pan and stir into the cooking liquid. Adjust the seasoning and reheat gently. Garnish with the fresh herbs.

SALADS
AND
VEGETABLES

Salads and vegetables can be served at almost any point in a French meal. You may find a selection of salads and cold vegetables to begin a summer lunch, simply cooked vegetables as a light appetizer, or perhaps golden, glazed root vegetables accompanying a roast. French cuisine has always recognized that using fresh seasonal ingredients is one of the keys to successful cooking and healthy eating, and it celebrates the best produce coming into the marketplace as the year unfolds.

CRUDITÉS

A colorful selection of raw vegetables, or crudités, *is often served in France as a quick and easy accompaniment to drinks or as small starters before lunch, especially in warm weather.*

The term *crudités* is used both for small pieces of vegetables served with a tasty dip and for a selection of vegetable salads presented in separate dishes. Country-style restaurants often feature a selection of *crudités* and sometimes a whole trolley of individual vegetables salads in small *raviers*, or shallow dishes, arrives. At a family lunch, at least two or three salads would be served. Their appeal lies in the use of fresh uncomplicated ingredients and a selection which offers visual and textural contrasts.

By choosing contrasting colors, any combination of vegetables, raw or lightly cooked, attractively arranged on a platter or in baskets and served with a tangy dip, such as *aïoli* or *tapenade*, can make a beautiful presentation. Allow 3–4 ounces of each vegetable per person. Remember, leftovers can be used in soups or a stir-fry. Add fruits, cold meats or seafood and a pretty herb or flower garnish – anything goes as long as you like it.

Aïoli (Garlic mayonnaise)

Put 4 crushed garlic cloves (or more or less to taste) in a small bowl with a pinch of salt and crush with the back of a spoon. Add 2 egg yolks and beat for 30 seconds with an electric mixer until creamy. Beat in 1 cup extra virgin olive oil, by drops until the mixture thickens. As it begins to thicken, the oil can be added in a thin stream until the mixture is thick. Thin the sauce with a little lemon juice and season to taste. Chill for up to 2 days; bring to room temperature and stir before serving.

Tapenade (Provençal olive paste)
Put 7 ounces pitted black olives, 6 anchovy fillets, 2 tbsp capers, rinsed, 1 or 2 garlic cloves, 1 tsp fresh thyme leaves, 1 tbsp Dijon mustard, juice of half a lemon, freshly ground black pepper and, if you like, 1 tbsp brandy in a food processor fitted with the metal blade. Process for 15–30 seconds until smooth, scraping down the sides of the bowl. With the machine running, slowly pour in 4–6 tbsp extra virgin olive oil to make a smooth firm paste. Store in an airtight container.

Raw Vegetable Platter
Assiette de crudités

SERVES 6–8
2 red and yellow bell peppers, sliced lengthwise
8 ounces fresh baby corn, blanched
1 chicory head (red or white), trimmed and leaves separated
6–8 ounces thin asparagus, trimmed and blanched
small bunch radishes with small leaves attached, washed
6 ounces cherry tomatoes, washed
12 quail's eggs, boiled for 3 minutes, drained, refreshed and peeled
aïoli *or* tapenade, *for dipping*

Arrange a selection of prepared vegetables, such as those above, on a serving plate. Cover with a damp dish towel until ready to serve.

Tomato and Cucumber Salad
Salade de tomates et concombre

SERVES 4–6
1 medium cucumber, peeled and thinly sliced
2 tbsp white wine vinegar
⅓ cup crème fraîche or sour cream
2 tbsp chopped fresh mint
4 or 5 ripe tomatoes, sliced
salt and freshly ground black pepper

Arrange the tomato slices on a serving plate, sprinkle with the remaining vinegar, and spoon the cucumber slices into the center.

Place the cucumber in a bowl, sprinkle with a little salt and 1 tbsp of the vinegar and toss with 5 or 6 ice cubes. Chill for 1 hour to crisp, then rinse, drain and pat dry. Return to the bowl, add the cream, pepper and mint and stir to mix well.

Carrot and Orange Salad
Carottes rapées à l'orange

SERVES 4–6
1 garlic clove, crushed
grated rind and juice of 1 large orange
2–3 tbsp grapeseed or peanut oil
*1 pound carrots, cut into very fine
   julienne strips*
2–3 tbsp chopped fresh parsley
salt and freshly ground black pepper

Rub a bowl with the garlic and leave in the bowl. Add the orange rind and juice and salt and pepper. Whisk in the oil until blended then remove the garlic. Add the carrots, half of the parsley and toss well. Garnish with the remaining parsley

MIXED GREEN SALAD

Salade de Mesclun

Mesclun is a ready-mixed Provençal green salad composed of several kinds of salad greens and herbs. A typical combination might include arugula, radicchio, lamb's lettuce and curly endive with herbs such as chervil, basil, parsley and tarragon.

<u>SERVES 4–6</u>

1 garlic clove, peeled
2 tbsp red wine or sherry vinegar
1 tsp Dijon mustard (optional)
5–8 tbsp extra virgin olive oil
7–8 ounces mixed salad greens and herbs
salt and freshly ground black pepper

1 Rub a large salad bowl with the garlic clove and leave in the bowl.

2 ▼ Add the vinegar, salt and pepper and mustard, if using. Stir to mix the ingredients and dissolve the salt, then whisk in the oil slowly.

VARIATION

Mesclun always contains some pungent leaves. When dandelion leaves are in season, they are usually found in the mixture, so use them when available.

---

3 ▲ Remove the garlic clove and stir the vinaigrette to combine. Add the greens and herbs to the bowl and toss well. Serve the salad at once.

APPLE AND CELERY ROOT SALAD

Pommes et Celeriac Remoulade

Celery root, despite its coarse appearance, has a sweet and subtle flavor. Traditionally parboiled in lemony water, in this salad it is served raw, allowing its unique taste and texture to come through.

<u>SERVES 3–4</u>

1 celery root (about 1½ pounds), peeled
2–3 tsp lemon juice
1 tsp walnut oil (optional)
1 apple
3 tbsp mayonnaise
2 tsp Dijon mustard
1 tbsp chopped fresh parsley
salt and freshly ground black pepper

1 Using a food processor or coarse cheese grater, shred the celery root. Alternatively, cut it into very thin julienne strips. Place the celery root in a bowl and sprinkle with the lemon juice and the walnut oil, if using. Stir well to mix.

2 ▲ Peel the apple, if you like, and cut into quarters and remove the core. Slice thinly crosswise and toss with the celery root.

3 ▼ Mix together the mayonnaise, mustard, parsley and salt and pepper to taste. Stir into the celery root mixture and mix well. Chill for several hours until ready to serve.

MUSHROOM SALAD   *Salade de Champignons à la Crème*

This simple refreshing salad is often served as part of a selection of vegetable salads, or crudités. *Letting it stand before serving brings out the inherent sweetness of the mushrooms.*

SERVES 4

6 ounces white mushrooms, trimmed
grated rind and juice of ½ lemon
about 2–3 tbsp crème fraîche or
     sour cream
salt and white pepper
1 tbsp snipped fresh chives,
     to garnish

VARIATION

If you prefer, toss the mushrooms
in a little vinaigrette – made by
whisking 4 tbsp walnut oil or
extra virgin olive oil into
the lemon juice.

1 ▼ Slice the mushrooms thinly and place in a bowl. Add the lemon rind and juice and the cream, adding a little more cream if needed. Stir gently to mix, then season with salt and pepper.

2 ▲ Let the salad stand for at least 1 hour, stirring occasionally.

3 Sprinkle the salad with snipped chives before serving.

LAMB'S LETTUCE AND BEETS   *Salade de Mache aux Betteraves*

This salad makes a colorful and unusual starter – the delicate flavor of the lamb's lettuce is perfect with the tangyness of the beets. If you like, sprinkle with chopped walnuts before serving.

SERVES 4

3–4 cups lamb's lettuce, washed and
     roots trimmed
3 or 4 small beets, cooked, peeled and
     diced
2 tbsp chopped fresh parsley
FOR THE VINAIGRETTE
2–3 tbsp white wine vinegar or
     lemon juice
1 heaping tbsp Dijon mustard
2 garlic cloves, finely chopped
½ tsp sugar
½ cup sunflower or grapeseed oil
½ cup crème fraîche or heavy cream
salt and freshly ground black pepper

1 First make the vinaigrette. Mix the vinegar or lemon juice, mustard, garlic, sugar, salt and pepper in a small bowl, then slowly whisk in the oil until the sauce thickens.

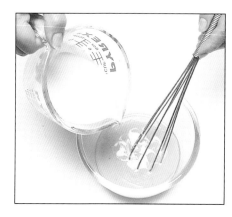

2 ▲ Lightly beat the crème fraîche or heavy cream to lighten it slightly, then whisk it into the dressing.

3 ▲ Toss the lettuce with a little of the vinaigrette and arrange on a serving plate or in a bowl.

4 Spoon the beets into the center of the lettuce and drizzle over the remaining vinaigrette. Sprinkle with chopped parsley and serve at once.

COMPOSED SALADS

Salade Composée

Composed salads make perfect starters. They are light and colorful and lend themselves to endless variation – and the components can often be prepared ahead for quick assembly.

The French are masters of the composed salad. Any combination of ingredients can be used – let your imagination and your palate guide you. Arranged attractively on a plate or in a bowl, this type of salad offers contrasting flavors, textures and colors. Raw or cooked vegetables, fresh fruits, hard-boiled chicken or quail eggs, smoked or cooked poultry, meat, fish or shellfish can all be used, but it is important that the dressing or other seasoning unite all the elements harmoniously.

Unlike a tossed salad such as *Salade de Mesclun*, in which the leaves are tossed together with a simple vinaigrette, the components of a composed salad are kept more separate. The ingredients might be arranged in groups, sometimes on a base of lettuce or other leaves, or simply arranged in circles on the plate. Composed salads, like *Salade Niçoise* or any of the following salads, are often served as a first course or a light main course, especially in warm weather. A tossed green salad is frequently eaten after the main course and is generally thought to clear the palate for the cheese course or dessert.

Shrimp, Avocado and Citrus Salad
Salade de crevettes aux agrumes

SERVES 6

1 tbsp fresh lemon juice
1 tbsp fresh lime juice
1 tbsp honey
3 tbsp olive oil
2–3 tbsp walnut oil
2 tbsp chopped fresh chives
1 pound cooked large shrimp, shelled and deveined
1 avocado, peeled, pitted and cut into tiny dice
1 pink grapefruit, peeled and segmented
1 large navel orange, peeled and segmented
2 tbsp toasted pine nuts (optional)
salt and freshly ground black pepper

Blend the lemon and lime juices, salt and pepper and honey in a small bowl. Slowly whisk in the olive oil, then the walnut oil to make a creamy sauce, then stir in the chopped chives. Arrange the shrimp with the avocado slices, grapefruit and orange segments on individual plates. Drizzle over the dressing and sprinkle with the toasted pine nuts, if using.

Smoked Salmon Salad with Dill
Salade de saumon fumé à l'aneth

SERVES 4

2 tbsp fresh lemon juice
½ cup extra virgin olive oil
2 tbsp chopped fresh dill, plus a few sprigs for garnishing
8 ounces smoked salmon, thinly sliced
1 fennel bulb, thinly sliced
1 medium cucumber, seeded and cut into julienne strips
black pepper
caviar, to garnish (optional)

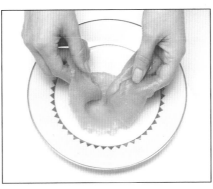

Arrange the salmon slices on four

individual plates and arrange the slices of fennel on top, then scatter the cucumber julienne over. Mix together the lemon juice and pepper in a small bowl. Slowly whisk in the olive oil to make a creamy vinaigrette. Stir in the chopped dill. Spoon a little vinaigrette over the fennel and cucumber slices. Drizzle the remaining vinaigrette over the salmon and garnish with sprigs of dill. Top each salad with a spoonful of caviar if desired.

Belgian Endive Salad with Roquefort
Salade aux endives et au Roquefort

SERVES 4

2 tbsp red wine vinegar
1 tsp Dijon mustard
¼ cup walnut oil
1–2 tbsp sunflower oil
2 Belgian Endive heads, white or red
1 celery heart or 4 celery stalks, peeled and cut into julienne strips
1 cup walnut halves, lightly toasted
2 tbsp chopped fresh parsley
4 ounces Roquefort cheese, crumbled
salt and freshly ground black pepper

Whisk together the vinegar, mustard, salt and pepper to taste in a small bowl. Slowly whisk in the walnut oil, then the sunflower oil. Arrange the endive on individual plates. Scatter the celery, walnut halves and parsley over. Crumble equal amounts of Roquefort cheese over each plate and drizzle a little vinaigrette over each.

WARM LEEKS WITH VINAIGRETTE *Poireaux Vinaigrette*

In France, leeks are sometimes called "poor man's asparagus," as they are cooked in similar ways and, like asparagus, are very good to eat. Use tender baby leeks if you can find them.

SERVES 6

12 small leeks (3 pounds)
2 hard-boiled eggs
1 tbsp Dijon mustard
2 tbsp white wine vinegar or lemon juice
6 tbsp sunflower oil
6 tbsp extra virgin olive oil, plus more
    if needed
salt and freshly ground black pepper
1–2 tbsp snipped fresh chives,
    to garnish

1 ▼ Remove the dark tough outer leaves of the leeks, then cut the leeks to the same length, and trim the dark green tops. Trim the root end, leaving enough to hold the leek together, then split the top half of the leeks lengthwise and rinse well under cold running water.

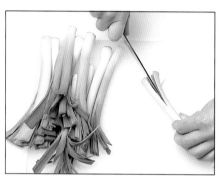

2 ▲ Lay the leeks flat in a large frying pan, pour over enough boiling water to just cover them and add a little salt. Cook the leeks over medium-high heat for 7–10 minutes until just tender. Carefully transfer to a large colander to drain, then lay the leeks on a paper towel and press them gently to remove as much liquid as possible.

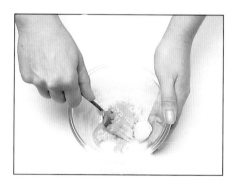

3 ▲ In a bowl, mash together the hard-boiled egg yolks and mustard to form a smooth paste. Season with salt and pepper and add the vinegar or lemon juice, stirring until smooth. Slowly whisk in the sunflower oil, then the olive oil to make a thick creamy vinaigrette.

4 Arrange the leeks in a serving dish and pour over the vinaigrette while the leeks are still warm. Chop the egg whites and sprinkle them over the leeks, then scatter over the snipped chives and serve warm or at room temperature.

FRENCH SCALLOPED POTATOES *Gratin Dauphinois*

These potatoes taste far richer than you would expect even with only a little cream – they are delicious with just about everything, but in France, they are nearly always served with roast lamb.

SERVES 6

2¼ pounds potatoes
3⅔ cups milk
pinch of ground nutmeg
1 bay leaf
1–2 tbsp butter, softened
2 or 3 garlic cloves, very finely chopped
3–4 tbsp crème fraîche or heavy cream
    (optional)
salt and freshly ground black pepper

1 ▲ Preheat the oven to 350°F. Cut the potatoes into fairly thin slices.

2 ▲ Put the potatoes in a large saucepan and pour over the milk, adding more to cover if needed. Add the salt and pepper, nutmeg and the bay leaf. Bring slowly to a boil over medium heat and simmer for about 15 minutes until the potatoes just start to soften, but are not completely cooked, and the milk has thickened.

3 ▼ Generously butter a 14 inch oval gratin dish or an 8 cup shallow baking dish and sprinkle the garlic over the base.

COOK'S TIP

If cooked ahead, this dish will keep hot in a warm oven for an hour or so, if necessary, without suffering; moisten the top with a little extra cream, if you like.

4 ▲ Using a slotted spoon, transfer the potatoes to the gratin or baking dish. Taste the milk and adjust the seasoning, then pour over enough of the milk to come just to the surface of the potatoes, but not cover them. Spoon a thin layer of cream over the top, or, if you prefer, add more of the thickened milk to cover.

5 Bake the potatoes for about 1 hour until the milk is absorbed and the top is a deep golden brown.

GLAZED CARROTS AND TURNIPS

Navets à la Nivernaise

In France when a dish is described on a menu as "à la nivernaise," it indicates the presence of carrots and onions. Here the addition of turnips adds a bittersweet contrast.

SERVES 6

3 tbsp butter
1 pound baby carrots, well-scrubbed, or medium carrots, cut into 1 inch sticks
1 pound young turnips, peeled and cut into quarters or eighths
½ pound pearl onions, peeled
½ cup beef or chicken broth or water
1–2 tbsp sugar
¼ tsp dried thyme
1–2 tbsp chopped fresh parsley

1 In a large heavy frying pan, melt 2 tbsp of the butter over a medium heat. Add the carrots, turnips and onions and toss to coat, then add the broth or water and stir in the sugar and thyme.

2 ▲ Bring the vegetables to a boil over medium-high heat, then cover and simmer over medium heat for 8–10 minutes until they begin to soften, shaking the pan occasionally to prevent the vegetables from sticking. Check the pan once or twice during cooking and add a little more liquid if needed.

3 ▼ Uncover the pan and increase the heat to evaporate any remaining liquid, stirring frequently, until vegetables are lightly coated with the glaze. Add the remaining butter and the chopped parsley to the pan and stir until the butter melts.

CREAMY SPINACH PURÉE

Purée d'Epinards

Crème fraîche, the thick French sour cream, or béchamel sauce usually give this spinach recipe its creamy richness, but try this quick, light alternative.

SERVES 4

1½ pounds leaf spinach, stems removed
4 ounces full- or medium-fat soft cheese
milk (if needed)
ground nutmeg
salt and freshly ground black pepper

1 Rinse the spinach, spin or shake lightly and place in a deep frying pan or wok with just the water clinging to the leaves. Cook, uncovered, over medium heat for 3–4 minutes until wilted. Drain the spinach in a colander, pressing with the back of a spoon to help extract the moisture; the spinach doesn't need to be completely dry.

2 ▼ In a food processor fitted with the metal blade, purée the spinach and soft cheese until well blended, then transfer to a bowl. If the purée is too thick to fall easily from a spoon, add a little milk, spoonful by spoonful.

3 ▲ Season the spinach with salt, pepper and nutmeg. Transfer the spinach to a heavy pan and reheat gently over low heat. Serve hot.

ZUCCHINI AND TOMATO BAKE

Tian Provençal

This dish has been made for centuries in Provence and it gets its name from the shallow casserole, tian, in which it is traditionally cooked. In the days before home kitchens had ovens, the assembled dish was carried to the bakery to make use of the heat remaining after the bread was baked.

<u>SERVES 4</u>

1 tbsp olive oil, plus more for
*   drizzling*
1 large onion (about 8 ounces), sliced
1 garlic clove, finely chopped
1 pound tomatoes
1 pound zucchini
1 tsp dried herbes de Provence
2 tbsp grated Parmesan cheese
salt and freshly ground black pepper

1 Preheat the oven to 350°F. Heat the oil in a heavy saucepan over low heat and cook the onion and garlic for about 20 minutes until soft and golden. Spread over the base of a 12 inch shallow baking dish.

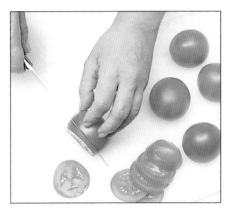

2 ▲ Cut the tomatoes crosswise into ¼ inch thick slices. (If the tomatoes are very large, cut the slices in half.)

3 Cut the zucchini diagonally into slices about ½ inch thick.

4 ▼ Arrange alternating rows of zucchini and tomatoes over the onion mixture and sprinkle with herbs, cheese and salt and pepper. Drizzle with olive oil, then bake for 25 minutes until the vegetables are tender. Serve hot or warm.

BAKED TOMATOES WITH GARLIC

Tomates à la Provençale

These tomatoes, epitomizing the flavor of Provence, are perfect with roast meat or poultry. You can prepare them a few hours ahead, then cook them while carving the roast.

<u>SERVES 4</u>

2 large tomatoes
3 tbsp dry breadcrumbs
2 garlic cloves, very finely chopped
2 tbsp chopped fresh parsley
2–3 tbsp olive oil
salt and freshly ground black pepper
flat leaf parsley sprigs, to garnish

1 Preheat the oven to 425°F. Cut the tomatoes in half crosswise and arrange them cut side up on a foil-lined baking sheet.

2 ▲ Mix together the breadcrumbs, garlic, parsley and salt and pepper and spoon over the tomato halves.

3 ▼ Drizzle generously with olive oil and bake the tomatoes at the top of the oven for about 8–10 minutes until lightly browned. Serve at once, garnished with parsley sprigs.

FISH
AND
SHELLFISH

Naturally lean and nutritious, seafood plays an important role in the exciting, enlightened style of French cuisine. The fresh briny aroma and delicate flavors of fish and shellfish are best preserved by simple, quick cooking methods such as steaming, broiling or pan-frying. Fruit, vegetables and herbs in almost limitless combinations offer an intriguing range of wholesome sauces and accompaniments to enhance fish and shellfish in a multitude of different ways.

TURBOT IN PARCHMENT

Turbot en Papillote

Cooking in parchment is not new, but it is an ideal way to cook fish. Serve this dish plain or with a little hollandaise sauce and let each person open their own package to savor the aroma.

SERVES 4

2 carrots, cut into thin julienne strips
2 zucchini, cut into thin julienne strips
2 leeks, cut into thin julienne strips
1 fennel bulb, cut into thin
*   julienne strips*
2 tomatoes, peeled, seeded and diced
2 tbsp chopped fresh dill, tarragon, or
*   chervil*
4 turbot fillets (about 7 ounces each), cut
*   in half*
4 tsp olive oil
4 tbsp white wine or fish stock
salt and freshly ground black pepper

1 ▼ Preheat the oven to 375°F. Cut four pieces of nonstick baking paper, about 18 inches long. Fold each piece of baking paper in half and cut into a heart shape.

2 ▲ Open the paper hearts. Arrange one quarter of each of the vegetables next to the fold of each heart. Sprinkle with salt and pepper and half the chopped herbs. Arrange two pieces of turbot fillet over each bed of vegetables, overlapping the thin end of one piece and the thicker end of the other. Sprinkle the remaining herbs, the olive oil and wine or stock evenly over the fish.

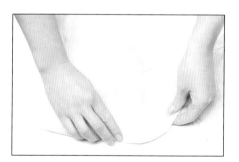

3 ▲ Fold the top half of one of the paper hearts over the fish and vegetables and, beginning at the rounded end, fold the edges of the paper over, twisting and folding to form an airtight package. Repeat with the remaining three. (The packages may be assembled up to 4 hours ahead and chilled.)

4 Slide the packages onto one or two baking sheets and bake for about 10 minutes, or until the paper is lightly browned and well puffed. Slide each package onto a warmed plate and serve immediately.

SALMON WITH GREEN PEPPERCORNS   *Saumon au Poivre Vert*

A fashionable discovery of nouvelle cuisine, green peppercorns add piquancy to all kinds of sauces and stews. Available pickled in jars or cans, they are great to keep on hand in your pantry.

SERVES 4

1 tbsp butter
2 or 3 shallots, finely chopped
1 tbsp brandy (optional)
4 tbsp dry white wine
6 tbsp fish or chicken broth
½ cup heavy cream
2–3 tbsp green peppercorns in brine,
    rinsed
1–2 tbsp vegetable oil
4 salmon fillets (6–7 ounces each)
salt and freshly ground black pepper
fresh parsley, to garnish

3 ▲ Reduce the heat, then add the cream and half the peppercorns, crushing them slightly with the back of a spoon. Cook very gently for 4–5 minutes until the sauce is slightly thickened, then strain and stir in the remaining peppercorns. Keep the sauce warm over very low heat, stirring occasionally, while you cook the salmon.

4 ▼ In a large heavy frying pan, heat the oil over medium-high heat until very hot. Lightly season the salmon and cook for 3–4 minutes, until the flesh is opaque throughout. To check, pierce the fish with the tip of a sharp knife; the juices should run clear. Arrange the fish on warmed plates and pour over the sauce. Garnish with parsley.

1 ▲ Melt the butter in a heavy saucepan over medium heat. Add the shallots and cook for about 1–2 minutes until just softened.

2 ▲ Add the brandy, if using, and the white wine, then add the broth and boil to reduce by three-quarters, stirring occasionally.

HALIBUT WITH TOMATO VINAIGRETTE   *Flétan Sauce Vièrge*

Sauce vièrge, *an uncooked mixture of tomatoes, aromatic fresh herbs and olive oil, can either be served at room temperature or, as in this dish,* tiède *(slightly warm).*

SERVES 2

3 large ripe beefsteak tomatoes, peeled,
    seeded and chopped
2 shallots or 1 small red onion, finely
    chopped
1 garlic clove, crushed
6 tbsp chopped mixed fresh herbs, such as
    parsley, cilantro, basil, tarragon,
    chervil or chives
½ cup extra virgin olive oil
4 halibut fillets or steaks
    (6–7 ounces each)
salt and freshly ground black pepper
green salad, to serve

1 ▼ In a medium bowl, mix together the tomatoes, shallots or onion, garlic and herbs. Stir in the oil and season with salt and freshly ground pepper. Cover the bowl and let the sauce stand at room temperature for about 1 hour to allow the flavors to blend.

2 ▲ Preheat the broiler. Line a broiler pan with foil and brush the foil lightly with oil.

3 ▲ Season the fish with salt and pepper. Place the fish on the foil and brush with a little extra oil. Broil for 5–6 minutes until the flesh is opaque and the top lightly browned.

4 ▲ Pour the sauce into a saucepan and heat gently for a few minutes. Serve the fish with the sauce and a green salad.

MUSSELS STEAMED IN WHITE WINE   *Moules Marinière*

This is the best and easiest way to serve the small tender mussels, bouchots, *that are farmed along much of the French coast line. In Normandy the local sparkling dry cider is often used instead of white wine. Serve with plenty of crusty French bread to dip in the juices.*

SERVES 4

4½ pounds mussels
1¼ cups dry white wine
4–6 large shallots, finely chopped
bouquet garni
freshly ground black pepper

1 ▲ Discard any broken mussels and those with open shells that refuse to close when tapped. Under cold running water, scrape the mussel shells with a knife to remove any barnacles and pull out the stringy "beards." Soak the mussels in several changes of cold water for at least 1 hour.

2 ▲ In a large heavy flameproof casserole combine the wine, shallots, bouquet garni and plenty of pepper. Bring to a boil over medium-high heat and cook for 2 minutes.

3 ▲ Add the mussels and cook, tightly covered, for 5 minutes, or until the mussels open, shaking and tossing the pan occasionally. Discard any mussels that do not open.

4 Using a slotted spoon, divide the mussels among warmed soup plates. Tilt the casserole a little and hold for a few seconds to allow any sand to settle to the bottom.

5 Spoon or pour the cooking liquid over the mussels, dividing it evenly, then serve at once.

VARIATION

For Mussels with Cream Sauce (*Moules à la Crème*), cook as above, but transfer the mussels to a warmed bowl and cover to keep warm. Strain the cooking liquid through a cheesecloth-lined colander into a large saucepan and boil for about 7–10 minutes to reduce by half. Stir in 6 tbsp heavy cream and 2 tbsp chopped parsley, then add the mussels. Cook for about 1 minute more to reheat the mussels.

PAN-FRIED SOLE

Sole Meunière

This simple recipe is perfect for fresh Dover sole and makes the most of its delicate flavor – lemon sole fillets are a less expensive, but an equally tasty alternative.

SERVES 2

*¾ pound skinless Dover sole or
    lemon sole fillets*
½ cup milk
⅓ cup flour
*1 tbsp vegetable oil, plus more
    if needed*
1 tbsp butter
1 tbsp chopped fresh parsley
salt and freshly ground black pepper
lemon wedges, to serve

1 ▼ Rinse the fish fillets and pat dry using paper towels.

2 ▲ Put the milk into a shallow dish about the same size as a fish fillet. Put the flour in another shallow dish and season with salt and freshly ground black pepper.

3 ▲ Heat the oil in a large frying pan over medium-high heat and add the butter. Dip a fish fillet into the milk, then into the flour, turning to coat well, then shake off excess.

4 ▲ Put the coated fillets into the pan in a single layer. (Do not crowd the pan; cook in batches, if necessary.) Fry the fish gently for 3–4 minutes until lightly browned, turning once. Sprinkle the fish with chopped parsley and serve with wedges of lemon.

SHRIMP WITH CURRY SAUCE · *Crevettes en Brochette à l'Indienne*

In France any dish called à l'Indienne *contains Indian spices. This sauce is great with broiled shrimp, but you can make it with chicken broth for serving with chicken, game, veal or pork.*

SERVES 4

16 large shrimp, peeled
grated rind and juice of 1 orange
juice of 1 lemon or lime
2 tbsp olive oil
1 garlic clove, crushed
1 tsp hot chili sauce or curry powder, or
   to taste
½ tsp ground coriander
½ tsp ground cumin

FOR THE CURRY SAUCE
1 tbsp olive oil
2 shallots, finely chopped
1 or 2 garlic cloves, crushed
1 tsp curry powder or paste
¼ tsp ground coriander
¼ tsp ground cumin
4 tbsp fish stock
1 cup heavy cream
1 tbsp chopped fresh cilantro
   or mint

1 ▲ Put the shrimp in a bowl with the orange rind and juice, lemon or lime juice, oil, garlic, chili sauce or curry powder, ground coriander and cumin. Stir well, then cover and marinate for 30 minutes.

2 To make the curry sauce, heat the oil in a medium saucepan over medium heat. Add the shallots and cook for 1–2 minutes, stirring, until just softened. Stir in the garlic and curry powder or paste, ground coriander and cumin and cook for 1–2 minutes, stirring constantly.

3 ▲ Add the fish stock and bring to a boil. Reduce by half, then add the cream and simmer for 8–10 minutes until slightly thickened. Stir in the fresh cilantro or mint. Reduce the heat to low and keep warm, stirring occasionally.

4 ▼ Preheat the broiler and line a broiler pan with foil. Thread the shrimp on to four metal or damp wooden skewers. Place the skewers on the broiling pan and broil for 3–4 minutes, turning once. Spoon a little sauce on to four plates. Place a skewer on each, and serve at once.

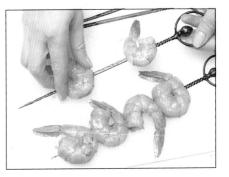

SEA BASS WITH CITRUS FRUIT

Bar Rôti aux Agrumes

Along the Mediterranean coast, sea bass is called loup de mer; *elsewhere in France it is known as* bar. *Its delicate flavor is complemented by citrus fruits and fruity French olive oil.*

SERVES 6

1 small grapefruit
1 orange
1 lemon
1 sea bass (about 3 pounds), cleaned and
    scaled
6 fresh basil sprigs
6 fresh dill sprigs
flour, for dusting
3 tbsp olive oil
4–6 shallots, peeled and halved
4 tbsp dry white wine
1 tbsp butter
salt and freshly ground black pepper
fresh dill, to garnish

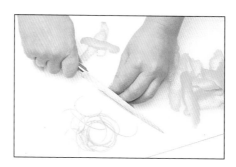

1 ▲ With a vegetable peeler, remove the rind from the grapefruit, orange and lemon. Cut into thin julienne strips, cover and set aside. Peel off the white pith from the fruits and, working over a bowl to catch the juices, cut out the segments from the grapefruit and orange and set aside for the garnish. Slice the lemon thickly.

2 Preheat the oven to 375°F. Wipe the fish dry inside and out and season the cavity with salt and pepper. Make three diagonal slashes on each side. Reserve a few basil sprigs for the garnish and fill the cavity with the remaining basil, the lemon slices and half the julienne strips of citrus rind.

3 ▲ Dust the fish lightly with flour. In a roasting pan or flameproof casserole large enough to hold the fish, heat 2 tbsp of the olive oil over medium-high heat and cook the fish for about 1 minute until the skin just crisps and browns on one side. Add the shallots.

4 Place the fish in the oven and bake for about 15 minutes, then carefully turn the fish over and stir the shallots. Drizzle the fish with the remaining oil and bake for 10–15 minutes more until the flesh is opaque throughout.

5 Carefully transfer the fish to a heated serving dish and remove and discard the cavity stuffing. Pour off any excess oil and add the wine and 2–3 tbsp of the fruit juices to the pan. Bring to a boil over high heat, stirring. Stir in the remaining julienne strips of citrus rind and boil for 2–3 minutes, then whisk in the butter. Spoon the shallots and sauce around the fish and garnish with dill and the reserved basil and grapefruit and orange segments.

MONKFISH WITH TOMATOES

Lotte à la Provençale

Monkfish was once scorned by fisherman because of its huge ugly head, yet now it is prized for its rich meaty texture – and is sometimes called "poor man's lobster."

SERVES 4

1¾ pounds monkfish tail, skinned and
    filleted
flour, for dusting
3–4 tbsp olive oil
½ cup dry white wine or fish stock
3 ripe tomatoes, peeled, seeded and
    chopped
½ tsp dried thyme
16 black olives (preferably Niçoise),
    pitted
1–2 tbsp capers, rinsed and drained
1 tbsp chopped fresh basil
salt and freshly ground black pepper
pine nuts, to garnish

1 ▲ Using a thin, sharp knife, remove any pinkish membrane from the monkfish tail. Holding the knife at a 45° angle, cut the fillets diagonally into 12 slices.

2 ▲ Season the slices with salt and pepper and dust lightly with flour, shaking off any excess.

3 ▲ Heat a large heavy frying pan over high heat until very hot. Add 3 tbsp of the oil and swirl to coat. Add the monkfish slices and reduce the heat to medium-high. Cook the monkfish for 1–2 minutes on each side, adding a little more oil if necessary, until lightly browned and the flesh is opaque. Transfer the fish to a warmed plate and keep warm while you make the sauce.

4 ▼ Add the wine or fish stock to the pan and boil for 1–2 minutes, stirring constantly. Add the tomatoes and thyme and cook for 2 minutes, then stir in the olives, capers and basil and cook for 1 minute more to heat through. Arrange three pieces of fish on each of four warmed plates. Spoon over the sauce and garnish with pine nuts.

POULTRY
AND
GAME

The natural leanness of poultry and game makes them an ideal component of successful, light cooking, and they are often quick to prepare, as well. Traditionally, a sauce accompanies a French main course, which adds immeasurably to its enjoyment. The recipes in this chapter include a wide range of simple, creative sauces with vibrant flavors to enhance a variety of poultry and game: both small, quickly cooked cuts and larger roast dishes.

CHICKEN WITH OLIVES

Poulet à la Provençale

Chicken breasts or turkey, veal or pork scallops may be flattened for quick and even cooking.
You can buy them ready-prepared in France, but they are easy to do at home.

<u>SERVES 4</u>

4 skinless boneless chicken breasts (about
*   5–6 ounces each)*
¼ tsp cayenne pepper
5–7 tbsp extra virgin olive oil
1 garlic clove, finely chopped
6 ripe plum tomatoes
16–24 pitted black olives
small handful fresh basil leaves
salt

1 ▼ Carefully remove the long finger-shaped muscle on the back of each breast and reserve for another use.

2 Place each chicken breast between two sheets of wax paper or plastic wrap and pound with the flat side of a mallet or roll out with a rolling pin to flatten to about ½ inch thick. Season with salt and the cayenne pepper.

3 Heat 3–4 tbsp of olive oil in a large heavy frying pan over medium-high heat. Add the chicken and cook for 4–5 minutes until golden brown and just cooked, turning them once. Transfer the chicken to warmed serving plates and keep warm while you cook the tomatoes and olives.

4 ▲ Wipe out the frying pan and return to the heat. Add another 2–3 tbsp of olive oil and fry the garlic for 1 minute until golden and fragrant. Stir in the olives, cook for 1 minute more, then stir in the tomatoes. Shred the basil leaves and stir into the olive and tomato mixture, then spoon it over the chicken and serve at once.

COOK'S TIP

If the tomato skins are at all tough, remove them by scoring the base of each tomato with a knife, then plunging them into boiling water for 45 seconds. The skin should simply peel off.

CHICKEN WITH RED WINE VINEGAR

Poulet au Vinaigre

This dish is an easy version of the modern classic invented by one of the masters of French cooking, the late Fernand Point of the Michelin-starred restaurant near Lyons, La Pyramide.

SERVES 4

*4 skinless boneless chicken breasts
    (7 ounces each)
4 tbsp unsalted butter
freshly ground black pepper
8–12 shallots, trimmed and halved
4 tbsp red wine vinegar
2 garlic cloves, finely chopped
4 tbsp dry white wine
½ cup chicken broth
1 tbsp chopped fresh parsley
green salad, to serve*

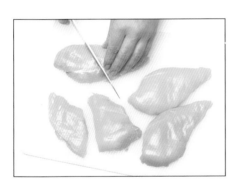

1 ▲ Cut each chicken breast in half crosswise to make eight pieces.

2 Melt half the butter in a large heavy-based frying pan over medium heat. Add the chicken and cook for 3–5 minutes until golden brown, turning once, then season with pepper.

3 ▲ Add the shallot halves to the pan, cover and cook over low heat for 5–7 minutes, shaking the pan and stirring the pieces occasionally.

4 ▲ Transfer the chicken pieces to a plate. Add the vinegar and cook, stirring frequently, for about 1 minute until the liquid is almost evaporated. Add the garlic, wine and broth and stir to blend.

5 Return the chicken to the pan with any accumulated liquid. Cover and simmer for 2–3 minutes until the chicken is tender and the juices run clear when the meat is pierced with a knife.

6 Transfer the chicken and shallots to a serving dish and cover to keep warm. Increase the heat and boil the cooking liquid until it has reduced by half.

7 Remove the pan from the heat. Gradually add the remaining butter, whisking until the sauce is slightly thickened and glossy. Stir in the parsley and pour the sauce over the chicken pieces and shallots. Serve at once with a green salad.

VARIATIONS

You could use different flavored vinegars. Try tarragon vinegar and substitute fresh tarragon for the parsley, or use raspberry vinegar and garnish with a few fresh raspberries.

ROAST CHICKEN WITH LEMON AND HERBS *Poulet Rôti*

In France, the evocative sight and smell of chickens roasting on their spits can often be found in charcuteries. A well-flavored chicken is essential – use a free-range or corn-fed bird, if possible.

SERVES 4

3 pound chicken
1 unwaxed lemon, halved
small bunch thyme sprigs
1 bay leaf
1 tbsp butter, softened
4–6 tbsp chicken broth or water
salt and freshly ground black pepper

COOK'S TIP

Be sure to save the carcasses of roast poultry for broth. Freeze them until you have several, then simmer with aromatic vegetables, herbs and water.

---

1 Preheat the oven to 400°F. Season the chicken inside and out with salt and pepper.

2 ▲ Squeeze the juice of one lemon half and then place the juice, the squeezed lemon half, the thyme and bay leaf in the chicken cavity. Tie the legs with string and rub the breast with butter.

3 ▲ Place the chicken on a rack in a roasting pan. Squeeze over the juice of the other lemon half. Roast the chicken for 1 hour, basting two or three times, until the juices run clear when the thickest part of the thigh is pierced with a knife.

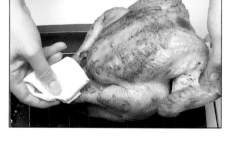

4 ▲ Pour the juices from the cavity into the roasting pan and transfer the chicken to a carving board. Cover loosely with foil and let stand for 10–15 minutes before carving.

5 ▲ Skim off the fat from the cooking juices. Add the broth or water and boil over medium heat, stirring and scraping the base of the pan, until slightly reduced. Strain and serve with the chicken.

DUCK WITH ORANGE SAUCE

Canard à la Bigarade

Commercially raised ducks tend to be much fattier than wild ducks. In this recipe, the initial slow cooking and pricking the skin of the duck helps to draw out the excess fat.

SERVES 2–3

4½ pound duck
2 oranges
½ cup superfine sugar
6 tbsp white wine vinegar or cider
    vinegar
½ cup Grand Marnier or orange liqueur
salt and freshly ground black pepper
watercress and orange slices,
    to garnish

1 ▲ Preheat the oven to 300°F. Trim off all the excess fat and skin from the duck and prick the skin all over with a fork. Season the duck inside and out with salt and pepper and tie the legs with string.

2 ▲ Place the duck on a rack in a large roasting pan. Cover tightly with foil and cook in the oven for 1½ hours. With a vegetable peeler, remove the peel in wide strips from the oranges, then stack two or three strips at a time and slice into very thin julienne strips. Squeeze the juice from the oranges.

3 ▼ Place the sugar and vinegar in a small heavy saucepan and stir to dissolve the sugar. Boil over high heat, without stirring, until the mixture is a rich caramel color, remove the pan from the heat and, standing well back, carefully add the orange juice, pouring it down the side of the pan. Swirl the pan to blend, then bring back to a boil and add the orange peel and liqueur. Simmer for 2–3 minutes.

4 Remove the duck from the oven and pour off all the fat from the pan. Raise the oven temperature to 400°F and return the duck to the oven.

5 ▲ Roast the duck, uncovered, for 25–30 minutes, basting three or four times with the caramel mixture, until the duck is golden brown and the juices run clear when the thigh is pierced with a knife.

6 Pour the juices from the cavity into the casserole and transfer the duck to a carving board. Cover loosely with foil and let stand for 10–15 minutes. Pour the roasting juices into the pan with the rest of the caramel mixture, skim off the fat and simmer gently. Serve the duck, with the sauce, garnished with watercress and orange slices.

CASSEROLED RABBIT WITH THYME *Fricassée de Lapin au Thym*

This is the sort of satisfying home cooking found in farmhouse kitchens and cozy neighbourhood restaurants in France, where rabbit is treated much like chicken and enjoyed frequently.

SERVES 4

2½ pounds rabbit
¼ cup flour
1 tbsp butter
1 tbsp olive oil
1 cup red wine
1½–2 cups chicken broth
1 tbsp fresh thyme leaves, or 2 tsp dried
    thyme
1 bay leaf
2 garlic cloves, finely chopped
2–3 tsp Dijon mustard
salt and freshly ground black pepper

1 Cut the rabbit into eight serving pieces: chop the saddle in half and separate the back legs into two pieces each; leave the front legs whole.

2 ▼ Put the flour in a plastic bag and season with salt and pepper. One at a time, drop the rabbit pieces into the bag and shake to coat them with flour. Tap off the excess, then discard any remaining flour.

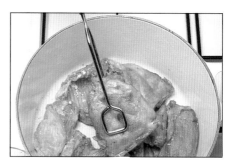

3 ▲ Melt the butter with the oil over medium-high heat in a large flameproof casserole. Add the rabbit pieces and cook until golden, turning to color evenly.

4 ▲ Add the wine and boil for 1 minute then add enough of the broth just to cover the meat. Add the herbs and garlic, then simmer gently, covered, for 1 hour, or until the rabbit is very tender and the juices run clear when the thickest part of the meat is pierced with a knife.

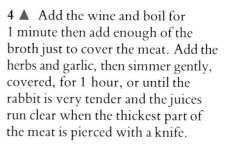

5 ▲ Stir in the mustard, adjust the seasoning and strain the sauce. Arrange the rabbit pieces on a warmed serving platter with some sauce and serve the rest separately.

PHEASANT BREAST WITH APPLES *Faisan à la Normande*

The Normandy countryside is full of picturesque apple orchards and herds of grazing cows. Many regional dishes contain apples or Calvados and rich Normandy cream.

SERVES 2

2 boneless pheasant breasts
2 tbsp butter
1 onion, thinly sliced
1 eating apple, peeled and quartered
2 tsp sugar
4 tbsp Calvados
4 tbsp chicken broth
¼ tsp dried thyme
¼ tsp white pepper
½ cup heavy cream
salt
sautéed potatoes, to serve

1 ▲ With a sharp knife, score the thick end of each pheasant breast.

2 In a medium heavy frying pan melt half of the butter over medium heat. Add the onion and cook for 8–10 minutes until golden, stirring occasionally. Using a slotted spoon, transfer the onion to a plate.

3 Cut each apple quarter crosswise into thin slices. Melt half of the remaining butter in the pan and add the apple slices. Sprinkle with the sugar and cook the apple slices slowly for 5–7 minutes until golden and caramelized, turning occasionally. Transfer the apples to the plate with the onion, then wipe out the pan.

4 ▲ Add the remaining butter to the pan and increase the heat to medium-high. Add the pheasant breasts, skin side down, and cook for 3–4 minutes until golden. Turn and cook for 1–2 minutes more until the juices run slightly pink when the thickest part of the meat is pierced with a knife. Transfer to a board and cover to keep warm.

5 Add the Calvados to the pan and boil over high heat until reduced by half. Add the broth, thyme, a little salt and the white pepper and reduce by half again. Stir in the cream, bring to a boil and cook for about 1 minute. Add the reserved onion and apple slices to the pan and cook for 1 minute.

6 Slice each pheasant breast diagonally and arrange on warmed plates. Spoon over a little sauce with the onion and apples.

COOK'S TIP

If you can't find Calvados, substitute Cognac, applejack or cider instead.

ROAST LEG OF VENISON

Gigot de Chevreuil Rôti

Although young venison does not need marinating to tenderize it, the marinade forms the base for a delicious, tangy yet slightly sweet sauce. You'll need to start this recipe two to three days ahead.

SERVES 6–8

1 onion, chopped
1 carrot chopped
1 celery stick, chopped
3 or 4 garlic cloves, crushed
4–6 fresh parsley sprigs
4–6 fresh thyme sprigs or ½ tsp
　dried thyme
2 bay leaves
1 tbsp black peppercorns, lightly
　crushed
3 cups red wine
4 tbsp vegetable oil, plus more
　for brushing
1 young venison haunch (about
　6 pounds), trimmed
2 tbsp flour
1 cup beef broth
1 unwaxed orange
1 unwaxed lemon
4 tbsp red currant or raspberry jelly
4 tbsp ruby port or Madeira
1 tbsp cornstarch, blended with 2 tbsp of
　water
1 tbsp red wine vinegar
fresh herbs, to garnish
French Scalloped Potatoes,
　to serve

1 ▲ Place the onion, carrot, celery, garlic, parsley, thyme, bay leaves, peppercorns, wine and oil in a deep glass dish large enough to hold the venison, then add the venison and turn to coat. Cover the dish with plastic wrap and leave to marinate in the refrigerator for 2–3 days, turning occasionally.

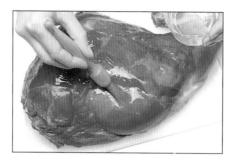

2 ▲ Preheat the oven to 350°F. Remove the meat from its marinade and pour the marinade into a saucepan. Pat the meat dry with paper towels, then brush the meat with a little oil on all sides and wrap tightly in foil.

3 ▲ Roast the venison for 15–20 minutes per 1 pound for rare to medium. About 25 minutes before the end of the cooking time, remove the foil, sprinkle the venison with the flour and baste with the cooking juices.

4 Meanwhile, add the broth to the marinade and boil over medium-high heat until reduced by half, then strain and set aside.

5 Using a vegetable peeler, remove the peel from the orange and half the lemon in long pieces. Cut the pieces into thin julienne strips. Bring a small saucepan of water to a boil over high heat and add the orange and lemon strips. Simmer them for 5 minutes, then drain and rinse under cold running water.

6 ▲ Squeeze the juice of the orange into a medium saucepan. Add the jelly and cook over low heat until melted, then stir in the port or Madeira and the reduced marinade and simmer gently for 10 minutes.

7 ▲ Stir the blended cornstarch mixture into the marinade and cook, stirring frequently, until the sauce is slightly thickened. Add the vinegar and the orange and lemon strips and simmer for 2–3 minutes more. Keep warm, stirring occasionally.

8 Transfer meat to a board and let stand, covered with foil for 10 minutes before carving. Garnish with herbs and serve with the sauce and French Scalloped Potatoes.

MEAT DISHES

Quickly sautéed or slowly simmered, these meat dishes deliver maximum satisfaction in great French style. Flavorful combinations of lean meats with herbs, vegetables and fruits make exciting lighter main courses for family suppers and special occasions. The selection includes options for veal and pork, especially lean meats, which are sometimes overlooked or misunderstood. Meat plays a vital role in creating a light, enjoyable way of eating.

PAN-GRILLED VEAL CHOPS · *Côtes de Veau à la Poële*

Veal chops from the loin are an expensive cut and are best cooked quickly and simply. The flavor of basil goes well with veal, but other herbs can be used instead if you prefer.

SERVES 2

2 tbsp butter, softened
1 tbsp Dijon mustard
1 tbsp chopped fresh basil
olive oil, for brushing
2 veal loin chops, 1 inch thick (about 8 ounces each)
salt and freshly ground black pepper
basil sprigs, to garnish

COOK'S TIP

If you prefer, replace the basil in the herb butter with fresh thyme or marjoram, or use a mixture of both. Or, omit the herb butter and top the veal chops with Tapenade.

1 ▲ To make the basil butter, cream the butter with the mustard and chopped basil in a small bowl, then season with pepper.

2 Lightly oil a heavy cast iron skillet. Set over high heat until very hot but not smoking. Brush both sides of each chop with a little oil and season with a little salt.

3 ▼ Place the chops on the skillet and reduce the heat to medium. Cook for 4–5 minutes, then turn and cook for 3–4 minutes more until done as preferred (medium-rare meat will still be slightly soft when pressed, medium meat will be springy and well-done firm). Top each chop with half the basil butter and serve at once.

VEAL SCALLOPS WITH TARRAGON · *Veau à l'Estragon*

These thin slices of veal need little cooking, and the sauce is made very quickly as well.

SERVES 4

4 veal scallops (about 4–5 ounces each)
1 tbsp butter
2 tbsp brandy
1 cup chicken or beef broth
1 tbsp chopped fresh tarragon
salt and freshly ground black pepper
tarragon sprigs, to garnish

1 Place the veal scallops between two sheets of wax paper or plastic wrap and pound with the flat side of a meat mallet or roll them with a rolling pin to flatten to about ¼ inch thickness. Season with salt and pepper.

2 ▼ Melt the butter in a large frying pan over medium-high heat. Add enough meat to the pan to fit easily in one layer (do not overcrowd the pan; cook in batches if necessary) and cook for 1½–2 minutes, turning once. (It should be lightly browned, but must not be overcooked.) Transfer to a serving platter or plates and cover to keep warm.

3 ▲ Add the brandy to the pan, then pour in the stock and bring to a boil. Add the tarragon and continue boiling until the liquid is reduced by half.

4 Return the veal to the pan with any accumulated juices and heat through. Serve immediately, garnished with tarragon sprigs.

VEAL STEW WITH TOMATOES

Sauté de Veau Marengo

The combination of tomatoes and orange in this dish brings to mind Mediterranean sunshine.

SERVES 6

4 tbsp flour
3 pounds boneless veal shoulder, cut into
　1½ inch pieces
2–3 tbsp olive oil
4 or 5 shallots, finely chopped
2 garlic cloves, very finely chopped
1¼ cups dry white wine
1 pound tomatoes, peeled, seeded and
　chopped
grated zest and juice of 1 unwaxed
　orange
bouquet garni
1 tbsp tomato paste
1 tbsp butter
¾lb button mushrooms, quartered if
　large
salt and freshly ground black pepper
chopped fresh parsley, to garnish

1 ▼ Put the flour in a plastic bag and season with salt and pepper. Drop the pieces of meat into the bag a few at a time and shake to coat with flour, tapping off the excess. Discard the remaining flour.

2 ▲ Heat 2 tbsp of the oil in a flameproof casserole over medium-high heat. Add enough meat to the pan to fit easily in one layer (do not overcrowd the pan or the meat will not brown). Cook, turning to color all sides, until well browned, then transfer to a plate. Continue browning the meat in batches, adding more oil if needed.

3 ▲ In the same pan, cook the shallots and garlic over medium heat, stirring, until just softened, then stir in the wine and bring to a boil. Return the meat to the pan and add the tomatoes, orange zest and juice, bouquet garni and tomato paste. Bring back to a boil, then reduce the heat to low, cover and simmer gently for 1 hour.

4 Melt the butter in a frying pan over medium heat and sauté the mushrooms until golden. Add the mushrooms to the casserole and cook, covered, for 20–30 minutes, or until the meat is very tender. Adjust the seasoning and discard the bouquet garni before serving. Garnish the stew with parsley.

ROAST LEG OF LAMB WITH BEANS
Gigot d'Agneau

Leg of lamb is the classic Sunday roast. In France, the shank bone is not removed, but it is cut through for easier handling. The roast is often served with green or fava beans.

SERVES 8–10

6–7 pound leg of lamb
3 or 4 garlic cloves
olive oil
fresh or dried rosemary leaves
1 pound dried navy or fava beans, soaked
    overnight in cold water
1 bay leaf
2 tbsp red wine
⅔ cup lamb or beef broth
2 tbsp butter
salt and freshly ground black pepper
watercress, to garnish

1 ▲ Preheat the oven to 425°F. Wipe the leg of lamb with damp paper towels and dry the fat covering well. Cut 2 or 3 of the garlic cloves into 10–12 slivers, then with the tip of a knife, cut 10–12 slits into the lamb and insert the garlic slivers into the slits. Rub with oil, season with salt and pepper and sprinkle with rosemary.

2 Set the lamb on a rack in a shallow roasting pan and put in the oven. After 15 minutes, reduce the heat to 350°F and continue to roast for 1½–1¾ hours (about 18 minutes per pound) or until a meat thermometer inserted into the thickest part of the meat registers 135–140°F for medium-rare to medium meat or 150°F for well-done.

3 Meanwhile, rinse the beans and put in a saucepan with enough fresh water to cover generously. Add the remaining garlic and the bay leaf, then bring to a boil. Reduce the heat and simmer for 45 minutes–1 hour, or until tender.

4 Transfer the roast to a board and stand, loosely covered, for 10–15 minutes. Skim off the fat from the cooking juices, then add the wine and broth to the roasting pan. Boil over medium heat, stirring and scraping the base of the pan, until slightly reduced. Strain into a warmed gravy boat.

5 ▼ Drain the beans, discard the bay leaf, then toss the beans with the butter until it melts and season with salt and pepper. Garnish the lamb with watercress and serve with the beans and the sauce.

61

LAMB STEW WITH VEGETABLES *Navarin d'Agneau Printanier*

A navarin is a stew made with lamb and a selection of young tender spring vegetables such as carrots, new potatoes, pearl onions, peas, green beans and especially turnips!

SERVES 6

4 tbsp vegetable oil
3 pounds lamb shoulder or other stewing
    meat, well trimmed, cut into 2 inch pieces
3–4 tbsp flour
4 cups beef or chicken broth
1 large bouquet garni
3 garlic cloves, lightly crushed
3 ripe tomatoes, peeled, seeded and
    chopped
1 tsp tomato paste
1½ pounds small potatoes, peeled if desired
12 baby carrots, trimmed and scrubbed
4 ounces green beans, cut into
    2 inch pieces
2 tbsp butter
12–18 pearl onions, peeled
6 medium turnips, peeled and quartered
2 tbsp sugar
¼ tsp dried thyme
1¼ cups peas
2 ounces snow peas
salt and freshly ground black pepper
3 tbsp chopped fresh parsley or cilantro,
    to garnish

1 Heat 2 tbsp of the oil in a large heavy frying pan over a medium-high heat. Add enough of the lamb to fit easily in one layer (do not overcrowd the pan or the meat will not brown). Cook, turning to color all sides, until well browned.

2 Transfer the meat to a large flameproof casserole and continue browning the rest of the meat in batches, adding a little more oil if needed. Add 3–4 tbsp of water to the pan and boil for about 1 minute, stirring and scraping the base of the pan, then pour the liquid into the casserole.

3 ▲ Sprinkle the flour over the browned meat in the casserole and set over medium heat. Cook for 3–5 minutes until browned. Stir in the broth, the bouquet garni, garlic, tomatoes and tomato paste and season with salt and pepper.

4 ▲ Bring to a boil over high heat, skimming off any foam that rises to the surface. Reduce the heat to low and simmer, stirring occasionally, for about 1 hour until the meat is tender. Cool the stew to room temperature, then chill, covered, overnight.

5 About 1½ hours before serving, take the casserole from the refrigerator and remove the fat from the surface, wiping the surface with paper towels to remove all traces of fat. Set the casserole over medium heat and bring to a simmer.

6 Cook the potatoes in boiling salted water for 15–20 minutes until tender, then using a slotted spoon, transfer to a bowl and add the carrots to the same water. Cook for 4–5 minutes until just tender and transfer to the same bowl. Add the green beans and boil for 2–3 minutes until tender, yet crisp. Transfer to the bowl with the other vegetables.

7 ▲ Melt the butter in a heavy frying pan or saucepan over medium-high heat. Add the onions and turnips with 3–4 tbsp water and cook, covered, for 4–5 minutes. Uncover the pan, stir in the sugar and thyme and cook, stirring and shaking the pan occasionally, until the onions and turnips are shiny and caramelized. Transfer them to the bowl of vegetables. Add 2–3 tbsp of water to the pan to deglaze and boil for 1 minute, scraping the base of the pan, then add this liquid to the lamb.

8 When the lamb and gravy are hot, add the reserved vegetables to the stew and stir gently to distribute. Stir in the peas and snow peas and cook for 5 minutes until they turn bright green, then stir in 2 tbsp of the parsley or cilantro and pour into a large warmed serving dish. Scatter over the remaining parsley.

RACK OF LAMB WITH MUSTARD   *Carré d'Agneau à la Moutarde*

This recipe is perfect for entertaining. You can coat the lamb with the crust before your guests arrive, and put it in the oven when you sit down for the first course.

SERVES 6–8

3 racks of lamb (7–8 ribs each), trimmed
   of fat, bones "French" trimmed
2 or 3 garlic cloves
4 ounces (about 4 slices) white or
   wholewheat bread, torn into pieces
1½ tbsp fresh thyme leaves or 1 tbsp
   rosemary leaves
1½ tbsp Dijon mustard
freshly ground black pepper
2 tbsp olive oil
fresh rosemary, to garnish
new potatoes, to serve

1 ▼ Preheat the oven to 425°F. Trim any remaining fat from the lamb, including the fat covering over the meat.

2 ▲ In a food processor fitted with the metal blade, with the machine running, drop the garlic through the feed tube and process until finely chopped. Add the bread, herbs, mustard and a little pepper and process until combined, then slowly pour in the oil.

3 ▲ Press the mixture onto the meaty side and ends of the racks, completely covering the surface.

4 Put the racks in a shallow roasting pan, and roast for about 25 minutes for medium-rare or 35 minutes more for medium (a meat thermometer inserted into the thickest part of the meat should register 135–140°F for medium-rare to medium). Transfer the meat to a carving board or warmed platter. Cut down between the bones to carve into chops. Serve garnished with rosemary and accompanied by new potatoes.

PORK TENDERLOIN WITH SAGE   *Filet de Porc à la Sauge*

Sage is often partnered with pork – there seems to be a natural affinity. The addition of orange brings complexity and balances the sometimes overpowering flavor of sage.

SERVES 4

2 pork tenderloins (about ¾ pound each)
1 tbsp butter
½ cup dry sherry
¾ cup chicken broth
2 garlic cloves, very finely chopped
grated zest and juice of 1 large orange
3 or 4 sage leaves, finely chopped
2 tsp cornstarch
salt and freshly ground black pepper
orange wedges and sage leaves,
*   to garnish*

1 ▼ Season the pork tenderloins lightly with salt and pepper. Melt the butter in a heavy flameproof casserole over medium-high heat, then add the meat and cook for 5–6 minutes, turning to brown all sides evenly.

2 Add the sherry, boil for about 1 minute, then add the broth, garlic, orange zest and sage. Bring to a boil and reduce the heat to low, then cover and simmer for 20 minutes, turning once until the juices run clear when the meat is pierced with a knife or a meat thermometer inserted into the thickest part of the meat registers 150°F. Transfer the pork to a warmed platter and cover to keep warm.

3 ▲ Bring the sauce to a boil. Blend the cornstarch and orange juice and stir into the sauce, then boil gently over medium heat for a few minutes, stirring frequently, until the sauce is slightly thickened. Strain into a gravy boat.

4 ▼ Slice the pork diagonally and pour the meat juices into the sauce. Spoon a little sauce over the pork and garnish with orange wedges and sage leaves. Serve the remaining sauce separately.

ROAST LOIN OF PORK WITH PRUNES *Rôti de Porc aux Pruneaux*

The combination of pork and prunes is often found in casseroles and stews from the Loire Valley, perhaps with one of the local wines. For the best flavor, soak the prunes overnight.

SERVES 6–8

18–24 prunes, pitted
3 cups fruity white wine, preferably
  Vouvray
4 pounds center cut pork loin (about 8
  ribs), backbone and skin removed
2 tbsp vegetable oil
1 large onion, coarsely chopped
1 large leek, sliced
2 carrots, chopped
1 celery stalk, sliced
2 tbsp brandy (optional)
1 cup chicken broth
bouquet garni
2–3 tbsp cornstarch, blended with 3 tbsp
  cold water
4 tbsp heavy cream
salt and freshly ground black pepper
watercress, to garnish
new potatoes, to serve

1 ▲ Put the prunes in a bowl, pour over the wine, then cover and let soak for several hours or overnight.

COOK'S TIP

It is important that the pork isn't overcooked – so for accurate timing, use a meat thermometer. Insert it into a fleshy part of the meat away from bones before roasting, or if using an instant-read thermometer, insert toward the end of cooking, following the manufacturer's instructions.

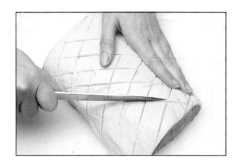

2 ▲ Preheat the oven to 400°F. Wipe the meat with damp paper towels, then dry the fat thoroughly. Score the surface of the fat with a sharp knife.

3 In a flameproof casserole or large heavy roasting pan, heat the oil over high heat until hot. Add the onion, leek, carrot and celery and cook for 3–5 minutes until browned, stirring frequently. Add the brandy, if using, broth and bouquet garni and stir well.

4 ▲ Put the pork on top of the vegetables and place in the oven. Roast for about 1½ hours until the juices run clear when the meat is pierced with a skewer, or a meat thermometer inserted into the thickest part of the meat registers 150°F. (If the liquid in the casserole or roasting pan evaporates, add a little of the prune soaking liquid or water to prevent the vegetables from burning.) Transfer the meat to a warmed serving platter, cover loosely with foil and let stand for 15 minutes.

5 ▲ Using a slotted spoon, transfer the prunes to a medium saucepan. Skim off as much fat as possible from the casserole or roasting pan and place over high heat. Add the prune liquid to the casserole or roasting pan and bring to a boil, stirring constantly and scraping the base. Boil for 3–4 minutes.

6 ▲ Stir the blended cornstarch into the casserole or pan and cook, stirring frequently for 2–3 minutes until the sauce thickens, then strain the contents of the pan into the saucepan with the prunes, pressing the vegetables to extract all the juice. Return the saucepan to medium heat, stir in the cream and simmer for 2 minutes, then season with salt and pepper. Reduce the heat to low and simmer gently, stirring frequently, until ready to serve.

7 Spoon the prunes onto the serving plate with a little of the sauce and pour the remaining sauce into a gravy boat. Garnish with watercress before serving with new potatoes.

LIGHT
PASTRIES
AND
CAKES

Pastries and cakes need not be eliminated in the quest for a lighter lifestyle. In fact, for many people, they are essential to its enjoyment. The key is moderation and adopting the French custom of reserving pastries and cakes for special celebrations or the occasional indulgent tea. The recipes in this chapter offer an array of exciting options for fabulous fruit tarts, tempting cookies and tender, fruit-filled cakes, to satisfy your sweet tooth.

APPLE TART

Tarte aux Pommes

This easy-to-make apple tart has rustic charm – it is just as you might find in a French farmhouse. Cooking the apples before putting them on the pastry prevents a soggy crust.

SERVES 6

2 pounds medium cooking apples,
   peeled, quartered and cored
1 tbsp lemon juice
¼ cup superfine sugar
4 tbsp butter
¾ pound shortcrust or sweet pastry (pâte
   sucrée)
crème fraîche or lightly whipped cream,
   to serve

VARIATION

For Spiced Pear Tart, substitute
pears for the apples, cooking them
for about 10 minutes until golden.
Sprinkle with ½ tsp ground
cinnamon and a pinch of ground
cloves and stir to combine before
arranging on the pastry.

---

1 Cut each cooking apple quarter lengthwise into two or three slices. Sprinkle with lemon juice and sugar and toss to combine.

2 ▲ Melt the butter in a large heavy frying pan over medium heat and add the apples. Cook, stirring frequently, for about 12 minutes until the apples are just golden brown. Remove the frying pan from the heat and set aside. Preheat the oven to 375°F.

3 ▲ On a lightly floured surface, roll out the pastry to a 12 inch round and trim the edge if uneven. Carefully transfer the pastry round to a baking sheet.

4 ▲ Spoon the apple slices onto the pastry round, heaping them up, and leaving a 2 inch border all around the edge of the pastry.

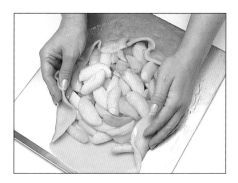

5 ▲ Turn up the pastry border and gather it around the apples to enclose the outside apples. Bake the tart for 35–40 minutes until the pastry is crisp and browned. Serve warm, with crème fraîche or cream.

NECTARINE PUFF PASTRY TARTS   *Tartes Feuilletées aux Nectarines*

These simple fresh fruit pastries are easy to put together, but the puff pastry makes them seem very elegant. You could use peaches, apples or pears instead of nectarines.

SERVES 4

½ pound puff pastry
1 pound nectarines
1 tbsp butter
2 tbsp superfine sugar
ground nutmeg
crème fraîche or lightly whipped cream, to serve (optional)

1 Lightly butter a large baking sheet and sprinkle very lightly with water.

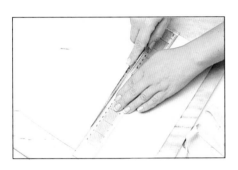

2 ▲ On a lightly floured surface, roll out the puff pastry to a large rectangle, about 15×10 inch and cut into six smaller rectangles.

3 ▲ Transfer to the baking sheet. Using the back of a small knife, scallop the edges of the pastry. Then using the tip of the knife, score a line ½ inch from the edge of each rectangle to form a border. Chill for 30 minutes. Preheat the oven to 400°F.

4 ▼ Cut the nectarines in half and remove the pits, then slice the fruit thinly. Arrange the nectarine slices down the center of the rectangles, leaving the border uncovered. Sprinkle the fruit with the sugar and a little ground nutmeg.

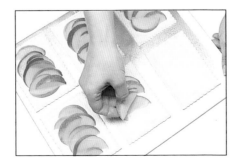

5 Bake for 12–15 minutes until the edges of the pastry are puffed and the fruit is tender.

6 Transfer the tarts to a wire rack to cool slightly. Serve warm with a little cream, if you like.

COOK'S TIP

These free-form puff pastry tarts can be made in other shapes, if you wish. Cut them in diamond shapes instead of rectangles, or cut into rounds, using a large cutter or a plate as a guide. Be sure to leave a border to allow the pastry to rise.

STRAWBERRY TART

Tarte aux Fraises

This tart is best assembled just before serving, but you can bake the pastry shell early in the day, make the filling ahead and put it together in a few minutes.

SERVES 6

¾ pound puff pastry
½ pound cream cheese
grated rind of ½ orange
2 tbsp orange liqueur or orange juice
3–4 tbsp confectioner's sugar, plus more for dusting (optional)
1 pound ripe strawberries, hulled

1 Roll out the pastry to about a ⅛ inch thickness and use to line an 11×4 inch rectangular flan pan. Trim the edges, neatly, then chill for 20–30 minutes. Preheat the oven to 400°F.

2 ▼ Prick the base of the pastry all over. Line the pastry case with foil, fill with baking beans and bake for 15 minutes. Remove the foil and beans and bake for 10 minutes until the pastry is browned. Gently press down on the pastry base to deflate, then leave to cool on a wire rack.

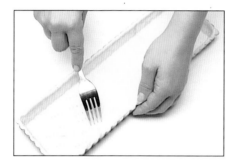

3 ▲ Using a hand mixer or food processor, beat together the cheese, orange rind, liqueur or orange juice and confectioner's sugar to taste. Spread the cheese filling in the pastry shell. Halve the strawberries and arrange them on top of the filling. Dust with sugar, if you like.

FRESH FRUIT TARTLETS

Tartelettes aux Fruits

These tartlets are so pretty filled with colorful fruit. Use a selection of whatever soft fruit is in season – cut large fruits into pieces that will fit easily into the tartlet cases.

SERVES 6

¾ pound shortcrust or sweet shortcrust pastry
4 tbsp apple jelly or raspberry jam
1–2 tbsp Kirsch or fruit juice
1 pound ripe small fruits (such as strawberries, raspberries, red currants, grapes, figs, kiwi fruit or apricots), hulled, pitted and sliced, as necessary

VARIATION

If you like, spoon a little flavored whipped cream into the pastry cases before filling with fruit. Whip about ½ cup heavy cream, sweeten to taste with confectioner's sugar and flavor with a little brandy or a fruity liqueur.

1 Preheat the oven to 400°F. Lightly butter six 3½in tartlet pans.

2 ▲ Roll out the pastry to about a ⅛ inch thickness. Using a tartlet pan, cut out six rounds, re-rolling trimmings as necessary. Use the pastry rounds to line the pans, then roll the rolling pin over the top of the pans to cut off the excess pastry. Prick the bases with a fork.

3 Line the pastry cases with foil and add a layer of baking beans. Bake for 15 minutes until slightly dry and set, then remove the foil and beans and continue baking for 5 minutes more. Cool on a wire rack.

4 ▲ Shortly before serving, melt the jam in a small saucepan over low heat with the Kirsch or fruit juice until melted. Arrange the fruit in the tartlet shells and brush all over with the glaze.

SPONGE CAKE WITH FRUIT AND CREAM *Génoise aux Fruits*

Génoise is the French cake used as the base for both simple and elaborate creations. You could simply dust it with confectioner's sugar, or layer it with seasonal fruits to serve with tea.

<u>SERVES 6</u>

¾ cup flour
pinch of salt
4 eggs, at room temperature
⅔ cup superfine sugar
½ tsp vanilla extract
4 tbsp butter, melted or clarified and cooled
FOR THE FILLING
1 pound fresh strawberries or raspberries
2–4 tbsp superfine sugar
2 cups whipping cream
1 tsp vanilla extract

1 Preheat the oven to 350°F. Lightly butter a 9 inch springform pan or deep cake pan. Line the base with nonstick baking paper, and dust lightly with flour. Sift the flour and salt together twice.

2 ▲ Half-fill a medium saucepan with hot water and set over low heat (do not allow the water to boil). Put the eggs in a heatproof bowl that just fits into the pan without touching the water. Using an electric mixer, beat the eggs at medium-high speed, gradually adding the sugar, for 8–10 minutes until the mixture is very thick and pale and leaves a ribbon trail when the beaters are lifted. Remove the bowl from the pan, add the vanilla extract and continue beating until the mixture is cool.

3 ▲ Fold in the flour mixture in three batches, using a balloon whisk or metal spoon. Before the third addition of flour, stir a large spoonful of the mixture into the melted or clarified butter to lighten it, then fold the butter into the remaining mixture with the last addition of flour. Work quickly, but gently, so the mixture does not deflate. Pour into the prepared pan, smoothing the top so the sides are slightly higher than the center.

4 ▲ Bake in the oven for about 25–30 minutes until the top of the cake springs back when touched and the edge begins to shrink away from the side of the pan. Place the cake in its pan on a wire rack to cool for 5–10 minutes, then invert the cake onto the rack to cool completely. Peel off the paper carefully.

5 ▲ To make the filling, slice the strawberries, place in a bowl, sprinkle with 1–2 tbsp of the sugar and set aside. Using an electric mixer or balloon whisk beat the cream with 1–2 tbsp of sugar and the vanilla until it holds soft peaks.

6 ▲ To assemble the cake (up to 4 hours before serving), split the cake horizontally, using a serrated knife. Place the top, cut side up, on a serving plate. Spread with a third of the cream and cover with an even layer of sliced strawberries.

7 Place the bottom half of the cake, cut side down, on top of the filling and press lightly. Spread the remaining cream over the top and sides of the cake. Chill the cake until ready to serve. Serve the remaining strawberries with the cake.

Macaroons

Macarons

Freshly ground almonds, lightly toasted beforehand to intensify the flavor, give these biscuits their rich taste and texture so, for best results, avoid using ready-ground almonds as a shortcut.

Makes 12

1⅓ cup blanched almonds, toasted
⅞ cup superfine sugar
2 egg whites
½ tsp almond or vanilla extract
confectioner's sugar, for dusting

1 Preheat the oven to 350°F. Line a large baking sheet with non-stick baking paper. Reserve 12 almonds for decorating. In a food processor fitted with the metal blade, process the rest of the almonds and the sugar until finely ground.

2 With the machine running, slowly pour in enough of the egg whites to form a soft dough. Add the almond or vanilla extract and pulse to mix.

3 ▲ With moistened hands, shape the mixture into walnut-size balls and arrange on the baking sheet.

4 Press one of the reserved almonds onto each ball, flattening them slightly, and dust lightly with confectioner's sugar. Bake the macaroons for about 10–12 minutes until the tops are golden and feel slightly firm. Transfer to a wire rack, cool slightly, then peel the cookies off the paper and leave to cool completely.

Cook's tip

To toast the almonds, spread them on a baking sheet and bake in the preheated oven for 10–15 minutes until golden. Cool before grinding.

Madeleine Cakes

Madeleines

These little tea cakes, baked in a special pan with shell-shaped cups, were made famous by Marcel Proust, who referred to them in his memoirs. They are best eaten on the day they are made.

Makes 12

1¼ cups flour
1 tsp baking powder
2 eggs
¾ cup confectioner's sugar, plus some for dusting
grated zest of 1 lemon or orange
1 tbsp lemon or orange juice
6 tbsp unsalted butter, melted and slightly cooled

Cook's tip

If you don't have a special pan for making *madeleines*, you can use a muffin pan, preferably with a nonstick coating. The cakes won't have the characteristic ridges and shell shape, but they are quite pretty dusted with a little confectioner's sugar.

1 Preheat the oven to 375°F. Generously butter a 12 cup madeleine pan. Sift together the flour and baking powder.

2 ▲ Using an electric mixer, beat the eggs and confectioner's sugar for 5–7 minutes until thick and creamy and the mixture forms a ribbon when the beaters are lifted. Gently fold in the lemon or orange zest and the lemon or orange juice.

3 ▲ Beginning with the flour mixture, alternately fold in the flour and melted butter in four batches. Let the mixture stand for 10 minutes, then carefully spoon into the pan. Tap gently to release any air bubbles. Bake the *madeleines* for 12–15 minutes, rotating the pan halfway through cooking, until a skewer inserted in the center comes out clean. Turn out onto a wire rack to cool completely and dust with confectioner's sugar before serving.

SAVARIN WITH SUMMER FRUIT

Savarin aux Fruits

This traditional dessert from Alsace-Lorraine is made from a rich yeast dough moistened with syrup and cherry liqueur. For babas au rhum, *the same dough can be baked in individual pans and soaked with rum syrup – either way it is quite delicious.*

SERVES 10–12

scant 1 tbsp active dry yeast
¼ cup superfine sugar
4 tbsp warm water
2¼ cups flour
4 eggs, beaten
1 tsp vanilla extract
7 tbsp unsalted butter, softened
1 pound fresh raspberries or strawberries
mint leaves, to decorate
1¼ cups whipping cream, sweetened to
*   taste and whipped, to serve*
FOR THE SYRUP
1¼ cups superfine sugar
2½ cups water
6 tbsp red currant jelly
3 tbsp Kirsch (optional)

1 ▲ Generously butter a 9 inch savarin or ring mould. Put the yeast and 1 tbsp of the sugar in a medium bowl, add the water and stir until dissolved, then leave the yeast mixture to stand for about 5 minutes until frothy.

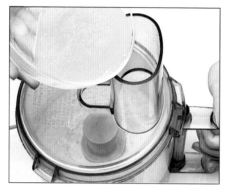

2 ▲ Put the flour and remaining sugar in a food processor fitted with the metal blade and pulse to combine. With the machine running, slowly pour in the yeast mixture, eggs and vanilla extract, then scrape down the sides and continue processing for 2–3 minutes, or until a soft dough forms. Add the butter and pulse about 10 times, until all the butter is incorporated.

3 ▲ Place the dough in spoonfuls into the mold, leaving a space between each mound of dough (this will fill in as the dough rises). Tap the mold gently to release any air bubbles, then cover with a dish towel and leave in a warm place to rise for about 1 hour. The dough should double in volume and come just to the top of the mold. Preheat the oven to 400°F.

4 Place the savarin or ring mold on a baking sheet in the oven and immediately reduce the temperature to 350°F. Bake for about 25 minutes until the top is a rich golden color and springs back when touched. Turn out the cake onto a wire rack and let stand to cool slightly.

5 ▲ To make the syrup, blend the sugar, water and 4 tbsp of the red currant jelly in a saucepan. Bring to a boil over medium-high heat, stirring until the sugar and jelly dissolve, and boil for 3 minutes. Remove from the heat and allow to cool slightly, then stir in the Kirsch, if using. In a small bowl, combine 2 tbsp of the hot syrup with the remaining red currant jelly and stir to dissolve. Set aside.

6 Place the rack with the cake, still warm, over a baking tray. Slowly spoon the syrup over the cake, catching any extra syrup in the tray and spooning it over the cake, until all the syrup has been absorbed. Carefully transfer the cake to a shallow serving dish (the cake will be very fragile) and pour over any remaining syrup. Brush the red currant glaze over the top, then fill the center with raspberries or strawberries and decorate with mint leaves. Chill, then serve with cream.

DESSERTS

The French can make a simple dessert
sensational, as this selection proves. Fresh
seasonal fruits, the jewels of the marketplace,
are the focus of many of these divine desserts,
characterized by a light touch and clever
combinations. As wholesome as it is tasty, fruit
provides an endless opportunity for making a
good thing even better. Savvy French ways
elevate essentially simple preparations to truly
memorable creations.

SIMPLE FRUIT DESSERTS

Les Fruits Frais

Weekday meals in a French home are likely to finish with fresh seasonal fruit – either a selection from the perpetually changing fruit bowl or an attractive yet simple-to-prepare fruit dessert.

Seasonal fruits can be made into tasty desserts quickly and easily. Each season produces its own special gems, strawberries in spring, peaches at the height of summer and apples, figs and citrus fruits in the fall and winter.

Some fruits seem to go particularly well with each other, while others are perfect partners to certain herbs and spices. For a classic fruit dessert, try a plate of fresh peach slices sprinkled with fresh raspberries; or sauté apple slices in butter, then sprinkle them with a little sugar and cinnamon and serve with yogurt. Do the same with pear slices, but sprinkle with a little sugar and ginger, then top with a spoonful of diced ginger and a dash of its syrup.

Oranges go well with just about everything. Segment a few oranges, saving the juice, combine the segments with sliced kumquats and sprinkle with pomegranate seeds for a simple yet stunning dessert.

Strawberries, raspberries and blueberries are best just as they are. If you like, sprinkle them with a little sugar, more for the crunch than anything else, or with a splash of orange liqueur or just some good fresh cream. Try flavoring the cream with a few crushed bay leaves, cardamom seeds or fresh mint leaves, then just pour over the fruit, or whip and serve separately. For a quick elegant dessert, spoon sliced or quartered strawberries into pretty dessert *coupes* or Champagne glasses, sprinkle with a little sugar and a dash of raspberry liqueur. Just before serving, pour over a little pink Champagne.

Melon and kiwi fruit slices look pretty together and are always refreshing. Serve ripe, aromatic mango slices on their own with a squeeze of lime juice or scatter over a few green or red grape halves to set off the color.

Fresh figs go well with juicy raspberries. For a more substantial dessert, cut a deep cross in the top of the figs and fill with a spoonful or two of cream cheese sweetened with honey and beaten with a little cream until fluffy. Sprinkle liberally with raspberries and douse with a little raspberry liqueur, if you like.

For fruit desserts, let the seasons, quality and a sense of color be your guide. You will find that fruits which are ripe at the same time are usually good together.

Fresh Pineapple with Kirsch
Ananas au Kirsch

SERVES 6–8
1 large pineapple
2 tbsp superfine sugar
2–4 tsp Kirsch or cherry brandy
mint sprigs, to decorate

Using a large sharp knife cut off the top and bottom of the pineapple. Stand the pineapple on a board. Cut off the peel from top to bottom using a small sharp knife, then lay the pineapple on its side and, following the direction of the eyes, use a sharp knife to remove them, cutting out a V-shaped wedge. You will end up with a spiral shape. Cut the pineapple into slices and use an apple corer or small round cutter to remove the tough central core, if you like. Arrange the slices on a large serving plate. Sprinkle evenly with sugar and Kirsch or cherry brandy. Chill until ready to serve, then decorate with mint sprigs.

Melon with Raspberries
Melons aux framboises

SERVES 2
2 tiny or 1 small ripe melon
1 cup fresh raspberries
1–2 tbsp raspberry liqueur (optional)

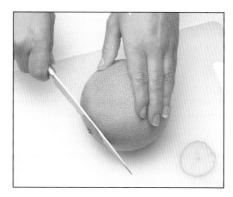

Cut off a thin slice from the bottom of each melon to create a stable base.

If the melons are tiny, cut off the top third and scoop out as much flesh as possible from each top. Cut the flesh into tiny dice. If a larger melon is used, cut off a thin slice from both the top and bottom to create two stable bases; then split melon in half. In either case, scoop out and discard seeds. Fill the center of the melon halves with the raspberries and, if you like, sprinkle with a little liqueur. Chill the melons before serving or serve on a bed of crushed ice.

Broiled Fruit Kebabs
Brochettes de fruits grillées

MAKES 4–6
4 or 5 kinds of firm ripe fruit, such as pineapple and mango cubes, nectarine and pear slices, grapes and tangerine segments
2 tbsp unsalted butter, melted
grated rind and juice of 1 orange
sugar, to taste
pinch of ground cinnamon or nutmeg
yogurt, sour cream, crème fraîche or fruit coulis, for serving

Preheat the broiler. Line a baking sheet with foil. Thread the fruit on to 4–6 skewers (soaked in water), alternating fruits to create an attractive pattern. Arrange the skewers on foil, spoon over the melted butter, orange rind and juice and sprinkle with the sugar to taste, together with a pinch of cinnamon or nutmeg. Broil for 2–3 minutes until the sugar just begins to caramelize and serve the kebabs at once with yogurt, sour cream or crème fraîche.

CREAM CHEESE WITH FRUIT SAUCE   *Coeur à la Crème*

This elegant yet simple to prepare dessert gets its French name, "hearts of cream," from the perforated heart-shaped molds they are traditionally made in.

SERVES 6–8

8 ounces cream cheese, softened
1 cup sour cream
1 tsp vanilla extract
about 3 tbsp superfine sugar, to taste
2 egg whites
pinch of cream of tartar
raspberries or other small fruit,
    to decorate
FOR THE PASSION FRUIT SAUCE
6 ripe passion fruits
1 tsp cornstarch blended with
    1 tsp water
4 tbsp fresh orange juice
2–3 tbsp superfine sugar, to taste
1–2 tbsp orange liqueur (optional)

1 ▲ Line six to eight *coeur à la crème* molds with cheesecloth. In a large bowl, beat the cream cheese until smooth. Add the sour cream, vanilla extract and sugar, beating the mixture until smooth.

2 In a clean greasefree bowl, using an electric mixer, beat the egg whites slowly until they become frothy. Add the cream of tartar, increase the speed and continue beating until they form stiff peaks that just flop over a little at the top.

3 Beat a spoonful of whites into the cheese mixture to lighten it, then fold in the remaining whites.

4 ▲ Spoon the cheese mixture into the molds, smooth the tops and place on a baking sheet to catch any drips. Cover the sheet with plastic wrap and chill overnight.

5 ▲ To make the sauce, cut each passion fruit in half crosswise and scoop the flesh and seeds into a medium saucepan. Add the blended cornstarch and stir in the orange juice and sugar. Bring the sauce to a boil over medium heat and simmer for 2–3 minutes until the sauce thickens, stirring frequently. Remove from the heat and cool slightly, then strain into a serving pitcher and stir in the orange liqueur, if using.

6 To serve, unmold the cheeses onto individual plates and remove the cheesecloth. Pour the fruit sauce around and decorate with fruit.

FRESH FRUIT WITH MANGO SAUCE   *Fruits au Coulis de Mangue*

Fruit sauce, coulis, *became fashionable in the 1970s with* nouvelle cuisine. *This bright, flavorful sauce is easy to prepare and ideal to make a simple fruit salad seem special.*

SERVES 6

1 large ripe mango, peeled, pitted
   and chopped
rind of 1 orange
juice of 3 oranges
superfine sugar, to taste
2 peaches
2 nectarines
1 small mango, peeled
2 plums
1 pear or ½ small melon
2 heaping tbsp wild strawberries
   (optional)
2 heaping tbsp raspberries
2 heaping tbsp blueberries
juice of 1 lemon
small mint sprigs, to decorate

1 ▲ In a food processor fitted with the metal blade, process the large mango until smooth. Add the orange rind, juice and sugar to taste and process again until very smooth. Press through a strainer into a bowl and chill the sauce.

2 Peel the peaches, if desired, then slice and pit the peaches, nectarines, small mango and plums. Quarter the pear and remove the core and seeds, or if using, slice the melon thinly and remove the peel.

3 ▼ Place the sliced fruits on a large plate, sprinkle the fruits with the lemon juice and chill, covered with plastic wrap, for up to 3 hours before serving. (Some fruits may discolor if cut ahead of time.)

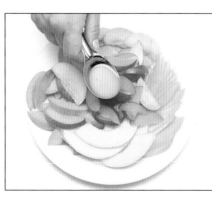

4 ▲ To serve, arrange the sliced fruits on serving plates, spoon the berries on top, drizzle with a little mango sauce and decorate with mint sprigs. Serve the remaining sauce separately.

FROZEN RASPBERRY MOUSSE
Crème Glaçée aux Framboises

This dessert is like a frozen soufflé. Freeze it in a ring mold, then you can fill the center with fresh raspberries moistened with framboise *or raspberry liqueur or just a little orange juice.*

SERVES 6

3 cups raspberries, plus more for serving
3 tbsp confectioner's sugar
2 egg whites
¼ tsp cream of tartar
½ cup granulated sugar
1½ tbsp lemon juice
1 cup whipping cream
15ml/1 tbsp framboise *or Kirsch*
mint leaves, to decorate

1 Put the raspberries in a food processor fitted with the metal blade and process until smooth, then press through a sieve. Or, simply work the raspberries through the fine blade of a food mill.

2 Pour a third of the purée into a small bowl, stir in the confectioner's sugar, then cover and chill. Reserve the remaining purée for the mousse.

3 ▼ Half-fill a medium saucepan with hot water and set over low heat (do not allow the water to boil). Combine the egg whites, cream of tartar, sugar and lemon juice in a heatproof bowl that just fits into the pan without touching the water. Using an electric mixer, beat at medium-high speed until the beaters leave tracks on the base of the bowl, then beat at high speed for about 7 minutes until the mixture is very thick and forms stiff peaks.

4 ▲ Remove the bowl from the pan and continue beating the egg white mixture for 2–3 minutes more until it is cool. Fold in the reserved raspberry purée.

5 Whip the cream until it forms soft peaks and fold gently into the raspberry mixture with the liqueur. Spoon into a 6 cup ring mold, then cover and freeze for at least 4 hours or overnight.

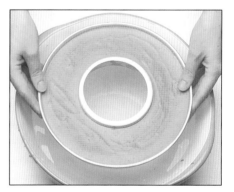

6 ▲ To unmold, dip the mold in warm water for about 5 seconds and wipe the base. Invert a serving plate over the mold and, holding it tightly against the mold, turn over together, then lift off the mold.

7 If you wish, fill the center of the mousse with raspberries, decorate with mint leaves and serve with the sweetened raspberry purée.

STRAWBERRIES WITH COINTREAU *Coupe de Fraises au Cointreau*

Strawberries at the height of the season are one of summer's greatest pleasures. Try this simple but unusual way to serve them. If you wish, use a mixture of fresh seasonal berries.

SERVES 4

1 orange
3 tbsp granulated sugar
5 tbsp water
3 tbsp Cointreau or orange liqueur
3 cups strawberries, hulled
1 cup whipping cream

1 ▲ With a vegetable peeler, remove wide strips of rind without the pith from the orange. Stack two or three strips at a time and cut into very thin julienne strips.

2 ▲ Combine the sugar and water in a small saucepan. Bring to a boil over high heat, swirling the pan occasionally to dissolve the sugar. Add the julienne strips and simmer for 10 minutes. Remove the pan from the heat and let the syrup cool completely, then stir in the Cointreau or liqueur.

3 ▼ Reserve four strawberries for decoration and cut the rest lengthwise in halves or quarters. Put them in a bowl and pour the syrup and orange rind over the top. Set aside for at least 30 minutes or for up to 2 hours.

4 ▲ Using an electric mixer or a whisk, whip the cream until it forms soft peaks. Sweeten to taste with a little of the syrup from the strawberries.

5 To serve, spoon the chopped strawberries into glass serving dishes and top with dollops of cream and the reserved strawberries.

BLACK CURRANT SORBET

Sorbet au Cassis

Black currants, which are prolific in Burgundy, make a vibrant and intensely flavored sorbet.

SERVES 4–6

½ cup superfine sugar
½ cup water
1 pound black currants
juice of ½ lemon
1 tbsp egg white

1 In a small saucepan over medium-high heat, bring the sugar and water to the boil, stirring until the sugar dissolves. Boil the syrup for 2 minutes, then remove the pan from the heat and set aside to cool.

2 ▼ Remove the black currants from the stalks, by pulling them through the tines of a fork.

3 In a food processor fitted with the metal blade, process the black currants and lemon juice until smooth. Alternatively chop the black currants coarsely, then add the lemon juice. Mix in the sugar syrup.

4 ▲ Press the purée through a sieve to remove the seeds.

5 ▲ Pour the purée into a shallow freezerproof dish and freeze until nearly firm, but still slushy.

6 ▲ Cut the sorbet into squares and put into the food processor. Process until smooth, then with the machine running, add the egg white and process until well mixed. Tip the sorbet back into the dish and freeze until almost firm. Cut the sorbet into squares again and process until smooth. Serve immediately or freeze, tightly covered, for up to 1 week. Allow to soften for 5–10 minutes at room temperature before serving.

CHOCOLATE SORBET

Sorbet au Chocolat

This velvety smooth sorbet has long been popular in France. Unsweetened chocolate gives by far the richest flavor, but if you can't track this down, then use the very best quality dark Continental plain chocolate that you can find or the sorbet will be too sweet.

SERVES 6

5 ounces unsweetened chocolate, chopped
4 ounces plain chocolate, chopped
1 cup superfine sugar
2 cups water
chocolate curls, to decorate

1 ▲ Put all the chocolate in a food processor, fitted with the metal blade and process for 20–30 seconds until finely chopped.

2 ▲ In a pan over medium-high heat, bring the sugar and water to a ·boil, stirring until the sugar dissolves. Boil for about 2 minutes, then remove from the heat.

3 ▼ With the machine running, pour the hot syrup over the chocolate. Allow the machine to continue running for 1–2 minutes until the chocolate is completely melted and the mixture is smooth, scraping down the bowl once.

4 ▲ Strain the chocolate mixture into a large measuring cup or bowl, and leave to cool, then chill, stirring occasionally. Freeze the mixture in an ice cream machine, following the manufacturer's instructions or see Cook's Tip (left). Allow the sorbet to soften for 5–10 minutes at room temperature and serve in scoops, decorated with chocolate curls.

COOK'S TIP

If you don't have an ice cream machine, freeze the sorbet until firm around the edges. Process until smooth, then freeze again.

ORANGES IN CARAMEL SAUCE

Oranges Caramelisés

The appeal of this refreshing dessert is the contrast between the sweetness of the caramel and the tangy tartness of the oranges. Made in advance, it is easy and convenient for entertaining.

SERVES 6

6 large unwaxed seedless oranges
½ cup granulated sugar

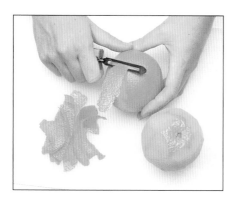

1 ▲ With a vegetable peeler, remove wide strips of rind from two of the oranges. Stack two or three strips at a time and cut into very thin julienne strips.

2 ▼ On a board, using a sharp knife, cut a slice from the top and the base of each orange. Cut off the peel in strips from the top to the base, following the contours of the fruit, then slice the peeled fruit crosswise into rounds about ½ inch thick. Put the orange slices in a serving bowl and pour over any juice.

3 ▲ Half-fill a large bowl with cold water and set aside. Place the sugar and 3 tbsp water in a small heavy saucepan without a nonstick coating and bring to a boil over high heat, swirling the pan to dissolve the sugar. Boil, without stirring, until the mixture turns a dark caramel color. Remove the pan from the heat and, standing well back, dip the base of the pan into the cold water to prevent the caramel cooking further.

4 ▲ Add 2 tbsp water to the caramel, pouring it down the sides of the pan, and swirl to combine. Add the strips of orange rind and return the pan to the heat. Simmer over medium-low heat for 8–10 minutes until they are slightly translucent, stirring occasionally.

5 Pour the caramel and rind over the oranges, turn gently to mix and chill for at least 1 hour.

Apple Charlotte

Charlotte aux Pommes

This classic dessert takes its name from the straight-sided pan with heart-shaped handles in which it is baked. The buttery bread crust encases a thick sweet, yet sharp apple purée.

Serves 6

2½ pounds apples
2 tbsp water
⅔ cup light brown sugar
½ tsp ground cinnamon
¼ tsp ground nutmeg
7 slices firm textured sliced white bread
5–6 tbsp butter, melted
custard, to serve (optional)

1 ▲ Peel, quarter and core the apples. Cut into thick slices and put in a large heavy saucepan with the water. Cook, covered, over medium-low heat for 5 minutes, and then uncover the pan and cook for 10 minutes until the apples are very soft. Add the sugar, cinnamon and nutmeg and continue cooking for 5–10 minutes, stirring frequently, until the apples are soft and thick. (There should be about 3 cups of apple purée.)

Cook's tip

If preferred, microwave the apples without water in a large glass dish on High (100% power), tightly covered, for 15 minutes. Add the sugar and spices and microwave, uncovered, for about 15 minutes more until very thick, stirring once or twice.

2 ▼ Preheat the oven to 400°F. Trim the crusts from the bread and brush with melted butter on one side. Cut two slices into triangles and use as many as necessary to cover the base of a 6 cup charlotte pan or soufflé dish, placing the bread triangles buttered-sides down and fitting them tightly. Cut the fingers of bread the same height as the pan or dish and use them to completely line the sides, overlapping them slightly.

3 ▲ Pour the apple purée into the pan or dish. Cover the top with bread slices, buttered-side up, cutting them as necessary to fit.

4 Bake the charlotte for 20 minutes, then reduce the oven temperature to 350°F and and bake for 25 minutes until well browned and firm. Let stand for 15 minutes. To turn out, place a serving plate over the pan or dish, hold tightly, and invert, then lift off the pan or dish. Serve with custard, if desired.

POACHED PEACHES WITH RASPBERRY SAUCE *Pêche Melba*

The story goes that one of the great French chefs, Auguste Escoffier, created this dessert in honor of the opera singer Nellie Melba, now forever enshrined in culinary, if not musical, history.

SERVES 6

4 cups water
¼ cup superfine sugar
1 vanilla bean, split lengthwise
3 large peaches
FOR THE RASPBERRY SAUCE
1 pound fresh or frozen raspberries
1 tbsp lemon juice
2–3 tbsp superfine sugar
2–3 tbsp raspberry liqueur (optional)
vanilla ice cream, to serve
mint leaves, to decorate

1 In a saucepan large enough to hold the peach halves in a single layer, combine the water, sugar and vanilla bean. Bring to a boil over medium heat, stirring occasionally to dissolve the sugar.

2 ▼ Cut the peaches in half and twist the halves to separate them. Using a small teaspoon, remove the peach pits. Add the peach halves to the poaching syrup, cut-sides down, adding more water, if needed to cover the fruit. Press a piece of wax paper against the surface of the poaching syrup, reduce the heat to medium-low, then cover and simmer for 12–15 minutes until tender – the time will depend on the ripeness of the fruit. Remove the pan from the heat and let the peaches cool in the syrup.

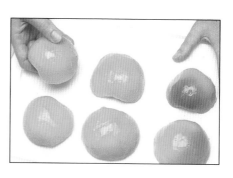

3 ▲ Remove the peaches from the syrup and peel off the skins. Place on several thicknesses of paper towels to drain (reserve the syrup for another use), then cover and chill.

4 ▲ Put the raspberries, lemon juice and sugar in a food processor fitted with the metal blade. Process for 1 minute, scraping down the sides once. Press through a fine strainer into a small bowl, then stir in the raspberry liqueur, if using, and chill.

5 To serve, place a peach half, cut-side up on a dessert plate, fill with a scoop of vanilla ice cream and spoon the raspberry sauce over the ice cream. Decorate with mint leaves.

COOK'S TIP

Prepare the peaches and sauce up to one day in advance. Leave the peaches in the syrup and cover them and the sauce before chilling.

CHOCOLATE SOUFFLÉS

Petits Soufflés au Chocolat

These soufflés are easy to make and can be prepared in advance – the filled dishes can wait for up to one hour before baking. For best results, use good quality bittersweet chocolate.

SERVES 6

6 ounces bittersweet chocolate, chopped
⅔ cup unsalted butter, cut in small pieces
4 large eggs, separated
2 tbsp orange liqueur (optional)
¼ tsp cream of tartar
3 tbsp superfine sugar
confectioner's sugar, for dusting
FOR THE WHITE CHOCOLATE SAUCE
6 tbsp heavy cream
3 ounces white chocolate, chopped
1–2 tbsp orange liqueur
grated zest of ½ orange

1 Generously butter six ⅓ cup ramekins. Sprinkle each with a little superfine sugar and tap out any excess. Place the ramekins on a baking sheet.

2 ▲ In a heavy saucepan over very low heat, melt the chocolate and butter, stirring until smooth. Remove from the heat and cool slightly, then beat in the egg yolks and orange liqueur, if using. Set aside, stirring occasionally.

3 Preheat the oven to 425°F. In a clean greasefree bowl, whisk the egg whites slowly until frothy. Add the cream of tartar, increase the speed and whisk until they form soft peaks. Gradually sprinkle over the sugar, 1 tbsp at a time, whisking until the whites are stiff and glossy.

4 ▼ Stir a third of the whites into the cooled chocolate mixture to lighten it, then pour the chocolate mixture over the remaining whites. Using a rubber spatula or large metal spoon, gently fold the sauce into the whites, cutting down to the bottom, then along the sides and up to the top in a semicircular motion until they are just combined. (Don't worry about a few white streaks.) Spoon into the prepared dishes.

5 ▲ To make the white chocolate sauce, put the chopped white chocolate and the cream into a small saucepan. Set over a low heat and cook, stirring constantly, until melted and smooth. Remove from the heat and stir in the liqueur and orange zest, keep warm.

6 Bake the soufflés for 10–12 minutes until risen and set, but still slightly wobbly in the center. Dust with confectioner's sugar and serve immediately with the sauce.

GLOSSARY

The following terms are frequently used in French cooking. In the recipes we have tried to reduce the use of technical terms by describing the procedures, but understanding these words is helpful.

BAIN-MARIE: a baking pan or dish set in a roasting pan or saucepan of water. It allows the food to cook indirectly and protects delicate foods; a double boiler is also a kind of water bath, or *bain-marie*.

BAKE BLIND: to bake or part-bake a pastry shell before adding a filling, usually done to prevent the filling making the pastry soggy.

BASTE: to moisten food with fat or cooking juices while it is cooking.

BEURRE MANIÉ: equal parts of butter and flour blended to a paste and whisked into simmering cooking liquid for thickening after cooking is completed.

BLANCH: to immerse vegetables and sometimes fruit in boiling water in order to loosen skin, remove bitterness or saltiness or preserve color.

BOIL: to keep liquid at a temperature producing bubbles that break the surface.

BOUQUET GARNI: a bunch of herbs, usually including a bay leaf, thyme sprigs and parsley stalks, used to impart flavor during cooking, often tied for easy removal.

CLARIFY: to make an opaque liquid clear and remove impurities; stocks are clarified using egg white, butter by skimming.

COULIS: a purée, usually fruit or vegetable, sometimes sweetened or flavored with herbs, but not thickened, used as a sauce.

CROÛTONS: small crisp pieces of fried or baked crustless bread.

DEGLAZE: to dissolve the sediment from the bottom of a cooking pan by adding liquid and bringing to a boil, stirring. This is then used as the basis for a sauce or gravy.

DEGREASE: to remove fat from cooking liquid, either by spooning off after it has risen to the top or by chilling until the fat is congealed and lifting it off.

DICE: to cut food into square uniform pieces about ¼in.

EMULSIFY: to combine two usually incompatible ingredients until smooth by mixing rapidly while slowly adding one to the other so they are held in suspension.

FOLD: to combine ingredients, using a large rubber spatula or metal spoon, by cutting down through the center of the bowl, then along the side and up to the top in a semicircular motion; it is important not to deflate or over-work ingredients while folding.

FOOD MILL *(mouli-légumes)*: tool for puréeing found in most French kitchens which strains as it purées.

GLAZE: to coat food with a sweet or savory mixture producing a shiny surface when set.

GRATINÉ: to give a browned, crisp surface to a baked dish.

HERBES DE PROVENCE: a mixture of aromatic dried herbs, which grow wild in Provence, usually thyme, marjoram, oregano and summer savory.

INFUSE: to extract flavor by steeping in hot liquid.

JULIENNE: thin matchstick pieces of vegetables, fruit or other food.

MACERATE: to bathe fruit in liquid to soften and flavor it.

PAPILLOTE: a greased non-stick baking paper or foil parcel, traditionally heart-shaped, enclosing food for cooking.

PARBOIL: to partially cook food by boiling.

POACH: to cook food, submerged in liquid, by gentle simmering.

REDUCE: to boil a liquid for the purpose of concentrating the flavor by evaporation.

ROUX: a cooked mixture of fat and flour used to thicken liquids such as soups, stews and sauces.

SAUTÉ: to fry quickly in a small amount of fat over a high heat.

SCALD: to heat liquid, usually milk, until bubbles begin to form around the edge.

SCORE: to make shallow incisions to aid penetration of heat or liquid or for decoration.

SIMMER: to keep a liquid at just below boiling point so the liquid just trembles.

SKIM: to remove froth or scum from the surface of stocks etc.

STEAM: moist heat cooking method by which vaporized liquid cooks food in a closed container.

SWEAT: to cook gently in fat, covered, so liquid in ingredients is rendered to steam them.

INDEX